TAPESTRIES

from the Renaissance
to the 19th century

Mercedes Viale

TAPESTRIES
from the Renaissance to the 19th century

CASSELL
LONDON

Cassell Publishers Limited
Artillery House, Artillery Row
London SW1P 1RT

Translated by Hamish St Clair-Erskine and Anthony Rhodes from the Italian
original
Gli arazzi

© Gruppo Editoriale Fabbri, Bompiani, Sonzogno, Etas S.p.A., Milan 1966,
1984

This edition 1988

British Library Cataloguing in Publication Data
Viale, Mercedes
Tapestries. — (Cassell's styles in art).
1. European tapestries, to 1966
I. Title   II. Gli arazzi. *English*
746.394

ISBN 0-304-32185-0

Printed in Italy by Gruppo Editoriale Fabbri S.p.A., Milan

CONTENTS

Page

INTRODUCTION

In the *Novo Dizionario Scolastico,* which was compiled
as long ago as 1892, 'tapestry' is described as 'an
ornamental cloth, woven with wool and gold thread,
telling a story'. The definition is more evocative than
precise; the words 'cloth' and 'gold thread' conjure
up a vision of something opulent, highly decorated
and unusual. The modern definition in the *Universal
Encyclopedia of Art* is 'a narrative woven into a fabric
with technical devices and detailed figures which
are different and distinct from the normal methods
used in fabrics for materials and carpets.' How
prosaic is this second version! They differ probably
because tapestries, produced all over the world today,
are familiar objects, whereas when Petrocchi penned
his definition, the manufacture had, as a living art,
clearly declined, and although still of great value,

had become primarily the preserve of aesthetes and scholars.

Between the end of the 18th and the early years of the 19th centuries, tapestry workshops gradually disappeared; those that survived could be counted on the fingers of one hand. Paradoxically, it was only then that the first documentary, historical and critical studies about tapestries appeared, beginning with those of Jubinal (1838, 1840). These were followed in quick succession by those of Barbier de Montault, Pinchart, Wauters, Müntz and Guiffrey. Italy contributed Conti, Campori, Braghirolli, Urbani de Gheltof, and Minieri Riccio. The avalanche of learned tracts, books and pamphlets which stimulated this interest appears directly related to the obsolescence of the craft itself.

We are told by writers like D'Annunzio that tapestries particularly excited the 'aesthetic sense . . . most subtle and powerful' of his hero Andrea Sperelli in his novel *Il Piacere*. His house overflowed with them—'the ancient tapestry that Giusto brought back from Flanders in 1508'—'the small Flemish tapestry woven with gold thread from Cyprus'—'the tapestries with the noble quarterings of the House of Sperelli'—'the finely spun Neapolitan tapestries' with 'Bacchic episodes of love'. There are pages more about it; nor is *Il Piacere* the only example. This theme occurs not only in D'Annunzio's works: in the more restrained manner of an Edoardo Calandra, we find a 'great panel of tapestry covering the whole wall', evoking the atmosphere and setting of a tale like *Le Masse Cristiane* (published the same year as *Il Piacere,* 1889) with admirable subtlety.

If antique *objets d'art* are really, as D'Annunzio wrote, comparable to 'a phial, which after long years retains the essence of the perfume it once contained', then tapestries must exhale a particularly heady scent, evoking tournaments, *'joyeuses entrées',* famous battles, conquering kings, rich merchants and great patrons of the arts—as well as depicting everything from overweening ambition to passionate love and dissolute gallantry. We may well ask why such a variety of subjects came within the scope of this woven art. Perhaps the answer is that in few other forms of aesthetic expression is there such a close association between the decorative and the social, the idealised or stylised and the purely mundane. Perhaps, too, because tapestries, owing to their cost and size, were essentially for the aristocracy, the 'fortunate few'. And so they would have remained, no more than a sign of their owner's wealth, had they not, with changing society and the collapse of values and shibboleths, taken on a distinct cultural significance, so that today an old tapestry seems to belong to a completely alien, vanished, yet fabulous era.

BIRTH OF THE TAPESTRY

The Origins

The subjects of the earliest tapestries of Western civilisation which we possess are not courts of chivalry and other profane splendour. Woven in the tranquil seclusion of the monasteries, among the arcades of Romanesque cloisters, they represent the patient work of the devout, dedicated to beautifying the house of God. The origin of the techniques themselves remains an enigma. Centuries before, the Copts wove narrative accounts into their panels in much the same way; it is possible that the invading Arabs appropriated their idea, from whom later the Crusaders acquired it. But this is pure hypothesis, without proof or evidence. We may as well admit our ignorance, and start with the first tapestry woven in the West which is known to us—the Cloth of St Gereon. The title of these fragments, which are scattered between the Kunstgewerbemuseum in Berlin, the Musée des Tissus in Lyon, the Victoria and Albert Museum in London and the National Museum in Nuremberg, is taken from the place of origin, the wonderful church of St Gereon in Cologne, where it hung in the choir. Some experts regard the work as oriental—a supposition as sound as any other if we agree that the art of tapestry is oriental. But this is not so; the decorative motif (a bull attacked by a gryphon, in medallions) derives from Sassanian textiles (already found in Cologne itself); but the ornamentation of the border and the background are of Western inspiration, remarkably similar to that in illustrated manuscripts of the 11th century. No other examples survive, until the panels in the cathedral of Halberstadt. The oldest—a strip depicting *Abraham and the Archangel Michael*—was probably woven about 1175. The strip depicting *Christ with the Apostles* can be dated one or two decades later, while the third—*Charlemagne among the Four Philosophers*—dates from the early years of the 13th century.

Early Techniques

In the St Gereon tapestry the decorative motifs are repeated identically at regular intervals over the entire surface. On the panels at Halberstadt there is, however, a definite change, which was to affect the future of Western tapestry. Historic figures appear here as a theme. Here are greater affinities with the sculptural elements of illuminated manuscripts, and an obvious connection with the artistic, cultural and historical school of Lower Saxony, where they were woven. The panel depicting Charlemagne can be compared with another woven work, the famous knotted carpet of Quedlinburg, from the studio of the convent of the Badessa Agnese, completed in about 1203.

There is no proof that the panel of Charlemagne was woven in this studio, but the similarity of the two works is clear: in the style (plastic sense, subtlety of design and variety of colour), and in the cultural content, the choice of 'learned' themes of classical inspiration. These themes, although carefully selected, are freely treated. The subject of the Quedlinburg carpet, the *Marriage of Mercury and Philology,* can be traced to a Latin text, reproduced by the 5th-century African rhetorician, Martianus Capella. Equally, Charlemagne's position as the fifth and most important sage of the Roman and Greek philosophers is not a profane glorification of the Emperor, but a pious metamorphosis of the great of antiquity into Christian heroes. Alexander the Great, Virgil and Trajan were later transmogrified in the same way.

The panel depicting Charlemagne is, unlike those already referred to, woven with a vertical instead of a horizontal warp. This was no doubt due to the difficulty of weaving strips of tapestry of unusual dimensions on a small loom. A fairly good idea of these old looms can be obtained from a 'trademark' in the workshop of a German convent, of much later date, but accurate enough, as the method of weaving remained almost unaltered during the Middle Ages. In the border of the *Passion* at Bamberg two nuns are seen at work. One is seated at an upright loom on which the threads of the warp are set (later these were unrolled from a beam placed at the top of the loom). The nun has already separated the even and uneven threads with sticks and fixed them to heddle strings, which allow her to alter their position. She then manipulates the spindles on which the threads of the weft are wound, divided as to colour and material (in those days only wool and flax—later, silk, silver and gold thread were used). The threads of the weft were then passed backwards and forwards between the two alternating series of warp threads which were thus entirely covered up. The nun works on what is to be the reverse of the tapestry, while her companion standing beside her compares the completed work with the design (or cartoon), which is placed at her side.

Looms of the same type were probably also used

in Norway. The most important document about the ancient manufacture of tapestry is the fragment of the *Months of April and May* (the remains of the decoration of a pew, once in the church of Baldishol, now in the Kunstindustrimuseet of Oslo). It is contemporary with the panel of Charlemagne, but its simplicity of form and colour are quite different from the subtle effects of the latter's more sophisticated treatment.

THE MIDDLE AGES

14th-Century Tapestries

There is now a large gap in our knowledge of tapestry: we possess only examples from the last quarter of the 14th century. At this date the art was largely diffused throughout Europe, each district with its own style and characteristics. Large studios flourished in Paris and Arras; more modest ones were active at Tournai; small workshops blossomed sporadically in Brabant, Hainault, Flanders, and neighbouring places. In Switzerland and Germany, groups of artisans produced strips and small panels for the local clientèle. Within the space of a hundred and fifty years, the art of tapestry had changed almost out of all recognition.

It is easy to explain how the technique of tapestry reached the Franco–Flemish countries. Never had travel been so extensive as in the Middle Ages. Emperors and popes, princes and knights, priests, pilgrims, merchants, strolling players and stone carvers were always on the move: and so no doubt were the tapestry weavers with their looms. It is harder to realise why anyone thought of transforming the occasional work of artisans into an industry, backed by a powerful financial organisation, and of adapting what had originally been intended as religious decoration to a flourishing secular industry. In early princely inventories *'tappiz de haulte lisse'* are only cursorily mentioned; but later more frequently. The vast halls of castles were decorated with ever larger and more luxurious hangings; tapestries served as screens to keep out the cold and wind. Then they invaded the bedrooms as canopies, and were spread out on benches and draped over chairbacks, finally becoming themselves veritable 'rooms'. So indispensable were these hangings that they accompanied their owners on journeys, and even went to war with them. Wear and tear in these circumstances was considerable, and they had to be renewed at considerable cost. These practical applications explain in part the favour they enjoyed, but they also had considerable prestige value. To own a tapestry was a sign of wealth, grandeur and power; and on public occasions, they were displayed ostentatiously as evidence of their owner's social importance.

Nor were the churches content with a few exiguous hangings: their walls were covered, and their naves partitioned, with tapestries. Dimensions increased, the spinning-mills poured out their *'fins filz'*, the carpenters constructed their looms, the weavers their warps—in a vast boom, which reached its peak at the end of the 15th century. In the early years of the

14th century Mahaut, Countess of Artois, was already buying tapestries as fast as she could. In Paris (where the *'tapissiers de haulte lisse'* had formed a competitive corporation in 1302) she began her purchases in 1308: in 1313 she was buying in Arras; and in Paris, in 1315 she acquired a panel *'à bestelets'*, consisting of animals woven probably on a decorated background. According to contemporary documents, a subject much sought after was the heraldic design or medallion.

The Illustration of Tales of Chivalry

Only towards the middle of the 14th century did tapestries have more complex designs, telling true stories in instalments as it were, each panel comprising a chapter, each series a complete tale, with its gallant precepts. Sometimes they were very long, like *Les Aventures des Enfans de Renaud de Montauban*. In the third quarter of the 14th century this type of story became firmly established. Charles V of France, Philip the Bold, Duke of Burgundy (from 1384 also Count of Flanders), Louis of Anjou and Jean de Berry were at that time the great patrons of the Parisian weavers: Nicolas Bataille (active *c.* 1368–1400), Pierre de Beaumetz (active *c.* 1382–1412) and Jacques Dourdin (active *c.* 1380–1407). Competition then started from Arras: Vincent Boursette (died 1376), Huart Walois, Colart d'Auxcy, Michel Bernard and Jehan Cosset. They were known as weavers, but were in fact 'employers of weavers'. The Boursettes and the Walois were prominent citizens of

Arras: Nicolas Bataille was *varlet de chambre* to the Duke of Anjou, and it would be hard to imagine them working at their looms.

The few surviving works of the 14th century are among the largest in the history of tapestry. Of the *Apocalypse of St John* only two-thirds remain (it was begun for Louis of Anjou between 1375 and 1377 in the workshops of Bataille). The preparation was long and detailed. The designer, Jehan de Bondolf or de Bandol, known as Hennequin de Bruges (hence, a Fleming), consulted illuminated manuscripts of the Apocalypse before undertaking the work. He is supposed to have gained little from them, because they could not convey the monumental mural sense, the length and breadth of a great wall surface. Yet the fact that they were consulted proves that tapestry was never (not even at that period) entirely free from the influence of other arts, painting in particular. Moreover these links were reciprocal: if the rhythm, gesture, cadence, and graphic forms of these arts were transmitted to tapestry, they returned to their sources renewed and transmuted. These many influences are bound up with those from other domains, from literature for example, so closely related to 'courtly' art. To this rightly belongs the series of the *Nine Heroes* with the arms of Jean de Berry (fragments in the Metropolitan Museum, New York). Woven about 1390, a little later than the *Apocalypse*, but probably by the same hand, it is not by the same designer and reveals a different inspiration—not so elevated, perhaps, and therefore more allied to its period, and above all to the search for a chivalrous and romantic ideal, as it then existed in the various courts. In the *Nine Heroes* the heroes of ancient and modern history and of mythology live together on an Olympus of Gothic splendour, from which the hardness of contemporary life cannot be entirely excluded. They are surrounded by the international language of cathedral spires, with backgrounds having the appearance of stained glass and weapons chiselled like reliquaries. Such elegant sugjects were addressed to the powerful and fortunate of that world, to a cavalier society in decline; yet they were destined still to be treated artistically in works of art created later in France, Flanders, Burgundy and Savoy.

Les Très Riches Heures (now at Chantilly) contains a miniature painted by the Limbourgs showing Jean de Berry at a banquet wearing an elaborate velvet costume trimmed with beaver, against a background borrowed from a tapestry depicting the feats of Bègue de Belin—an undulating line of lances, helmets, horses and warriors set in a landscape of gently rolling green hills. These subjects may have partly accounted for the popularity of the tapestry; purchasers identified themselves unconsciously, and somewhat inaptly, with these heroes, their adventures and conquests. Philip the Bold immediately commemorated the battle of Roosebeke, where Charles VI of France and Louis de Maële suppressed the Flemish revolt, with a tapestry which was woven in Arras by Michel Bernard. This exquisite work of art in wool, silk and gold thread was more than three hundred yards square. Charles VI did likewise when, in a tapestry by Jacques Dourdin and Nicolas Bataille, he commemorated the accolade bestowed on his brother the Duke of Orleans and his cousin Louis II of Anjou. This work *'toute d'imagerye d'or'*, was known as the *Joutes St Denis*. In these tapestries, which have not survived, the present must have seemed to join hands with an idealised past. We know that when the English won the battle of Agincourt and took Paris, the beautiful tapestries of Charles VI were looted.

ARRAS AND TOURNAI

The English Victory

Although the English victory was a blow to dreams and illusions, the myth of chivalry persisted. It persevered in Burgundy, whose Dukes commissioned their hangings from Arras. The only documented tapestries from Arras that have survived are the *History of St Piat and St Eleuthère* in the cathedral of Tournai (1402). The designs recount traditional tales of chivalry, but the stories are told with an everyday realism, which is almost middle class. In any case these tapestries were commissioned not by princes, but by the chaplain of the cathedral, Toussaint Prier. The weaver was Pierrot Féré, who was not in the front rank of great middlemen of Arras.

With the exception of the *History of St Piat and St Eleuthère*, we have no documentary evidence that any one tapestry came from Arras; we can only deduce this from common pictorial elements in certain works. The exquisite early 15th-century tapestry, *The Meeting of Fromon and Girart* (an episode from the *Saga of Jourdain de Blaye*) in the Museo Civico at Padua, is attributed to Arras, as are some of the *Scenes from Feudal Life* in the Musée des Arts Décoratifs in Paris, and the *Annunciation* in the Metropolitan Museum, New York, recalling something of the profundity as well as the tenderness of Broederlam. The same can be said for the superb *Crucifixion* in La Seo cathedral at Saragossa.

On a more solemn and monumental scale than in the *History of St Piat and St Eleuthère,* the Saragossa tapestry has the same realism; it deals with similar human emotions, affectionately, without any concession to the age of chivalry, or to the involved and decorative symbols associated with its art. These are to be found, however, in the Devonshire *Hunting Scenes* (Victoria and Albert Museum, London), which are believed to be from Arras, founded on miniatures of hunting scenes, with subtle half-tints of pink, violet and green. These belong to the second quarter of the 15th century. In the middle of that century, it became easier to attribute works to Arras or Tournai because there is documentary evidence of tapestries from the latter city.

Artistic and commercial relations between the two places were close, an Arras painter, Baudoin du Bailleul, furnishing them both with designs. And in both cities the same families of weavers had workshops. But the origin of some of the most important tapestries, whose peregrinations over Europe can be followed, remains uncertain. The *History of Clovis* in the cathedral of Rheims is an example; woven probably about 1450, it adorned the banqueting hall for the festivities celebrating the marriage of Charles the Bold with Margaret of York. The same can be said for the *History of St Peter* (now shared between Beauvais cathedral, the Musée de Cluny and the Museum of Fine Arts in Boston) which were commissioned by Guillaume de Hellande, Bishop of Beauvais, to celebrate the end of the Hundred Years War (1453).

There is no definite means of distinguishing between the tapestries of Arras and Tournai. This might have been possible, had the *Story of Gideon* been preserved; it was commissioned by Philip the Good to commemorate the installation of the Order of the Golden Fleece, and completed in 1453 by two weavers of Tournai, Jacques Dary and Jehan de l'Ortye, from cartoons of Baudoin du Bailleul. This series has been described in the ancient chronicles as 'the richest tapestry ever to adorn a royal court', a supreme testimonial to the luxury and pride of the Burgundian dynasty. As a memorial to their grandeur the *Story of Alexander the Great* still survives; flanked by the *Story of Gideon* it adorned the Hôtel d'Artois at the time of the *'joyeuse entrée'* of Louis XI into Paris (1461). These are now identified as the two tapestries in the Doria Pamphili Gallery in Rome. Then there is the *Story of the Swan Knight,* inspired by a performance of the *Voeu du Faisan* at Lille, in 1454; here the Burgundian knights, recalling the deeds of the mythical 'hero', the putative ancestor of the dynasty, vowed to repeat them, in combat with the enemies of the Faith. This series was woven at Tournai, perhaps in the great workshops of Pasquier Grenier.

The style of these tapestries and of certain others that are comparable is generally uniform and enables them to be attributed to Tournai (the *Battle of Roncesvalles* in the Bargello, Florence, and the Musées Royaux d'Art et d'Histoire, Brussels; the *Passion* in the Vatican and the Musées Royaux d'Art et d'Histoire, Brussels; the *History of Julius Caesar* in the Historisches Museum, Berne; the *Story of Tideo,* in the town hall of Madrid). The figures depicted are all prominently placed in the foreground clearly outlined, as if in the frame of a window. Even though the various episodes recounted took place at different times and in different places they are placed contiguously one next to the other in vertical disarray without any visible division. Bearing in mind that the tapestry was then regarded as a high 'woven wall', having little connection with the rules of perspective taught in the Renaissance, the presentation is perfectly logical.

It is difficult to say who invented this monumental treatment of serried figures. On account of their stylistic and historical elements, they have been attributed to the school of Robert Campin. Other comparisons, with miniatures, stained glass, sculpture and goldsmith's work, can be made; nor should a similarity with the so-called 'minor arts' patronised by those great lovers of the arts, the Dukes of Burgundy, be ignored. However, some definite attributions can be made. *The Legend of Herkenbald* in the Historisches Museum at Berne was a copy of the lost paintings of Roger van der Weyden which used to hang in the hôtel de ville in Brussels.

The literary sources are relatively easier to determine, thanks to the inscriptions which accompany each tapestry, commenting on and explaining the action. The whole literature of the late Middle Ages (including the theatre) was used. The themes vary from the miracles of Christ and the saints to exploits of valiant Carolingian knights; they deal with the even more remote and fabulous feats of Hercules and the Trojans, as well as with those from the classical story of Julius Caesar and Trajan, down to the relatively recent *Portuguese Conquests* of 1471 (in the collegiate church of Pastrana). The 15th-century tapestries comprise a kind of illustrated encyclopedia of the knowledge, ideals, daring deeds and productions of an aristocratic society which was overweeningly proud of its achievements and privileges. The court of Charles the Bold displayed in the Burgundian decline all its pomp and riches— ironically, in view of the political and military weakness of his dying regime. Although threatened by powerful enemies, the ambitious Louis XI of France and the hostile Swiss, Charles set out confidently on his campaign, taking with him his finest tapestries. Nemesis overtook him on the fields of Morat, Granson and Nancy. He fell in battle, and among the vast booty captured by his conquerors was the *Millefiori* (Thousand Flowers) bearing the Burgundian arms. This work, now in the Historisches

Museum, Berne, was woven in Brussels for his father Philip the Good.

If it is not strictly accurate to say that the tapestry centre of Arras, which gave its name to the art, disappeared with the Burgundian dynasty, after its destruction and sack (for the production continued to flourish at Tournai), the art itself was henceforth transformed. The live tradition of a knightly society was no longer represented in the work of the weavers. It is suitable, therefore, at this point to examine what was happening in the same field in Germany and Switzerland.

GERMANY AND SWITZERLAND

The weaving of small tapestries, for altar frontals and dossals, pew covers and cushions, continued in these countries throughout the 14th and 15th centuries. Sacred subjects were selected for the churches, scenes of everyday life, fables and popular allegories for private houses. The colours are vivid, and fresh, intended more for decoration than fidelity to nature. The design is stylised, again for decorative purposes, although even here the influence of pictorial art cannot be excluded.

These characteristics in common vary considerably from district to district. In the 14th century, the most important group of tapestries came from Constance. The Morgan *Crucifixion* in the Metropolitan Museum, New York, and the *Saints* in the German National Museum, Nuremberg, have a definite similarity of line and are set against a mono-chrome background, dotted with stars. Tapestries with medallions are common, the frontal hanging in Thun Museum being a good example in the first half of the 14th century.

Towards the end of the 14th century, the *Wilde Leute* make their appearance—wild-looking, hirsute men engaged in hunting and struggles with fantastic beasts, or holding placards inscribed with proverbs, maxims or moral texts. In the 15th century, especially in Basle, they dominate the scene. In Basle the scenes are mostly profane—hunting, gardens of love (*Minneteppiche*), monstrous animals (*Fabeltierteppiche*).

Around Freiburg and in northern Switzerland the subjects are more often sacred. The exquisite Gothic theme of the *Hortus Conclusus* occurs several times, sometimes combined with the *Mystical Chase*: both are interpreted in heraldic fashion, usually in fable form.

In Nuremberg the subjects were usually sacred. The strips of the *Life of St Sebaldus* (1410), the *Life of St Catherine* (1445) and the *Life of the Virgin* (1480) are inspired by the local school of painting. All these are in the National Museum, Nuremberg, and all were certainly woven in convents. The *Passion* in the cathedral of Bamberg, inspired by the famous *Passion* of Schongauer, was also woven in a convent; it is on a smaller scale, non-monumental, each of the nine episodes being in its own individual square. These are entirely different from Flemish tapestry com-position, whose influence began to be felt towards the end of the century in Germany, an example being the *Crucifixion* dated 1490 in the Würzburg Museum.

BRUSSELS AND ITS 'BELLE EPOQUE'

'Flemish tapestry', at the turn of the 15th and 16th centuries, meant primarily Brussels tapestry; the city had become the principal centre for tapestry weaving, with a technique and character quite unlike that in other workshops. Novel characteristics too were the search for technical perfection, recognisable in the earliest works attributed, probably rightly, to Brussels, and a bias towards painting. Today the design of a tapestry is often traced to a famous painting, as in the many representations of the *Baptism of Christ* (Kunsthistorisches Museum, Vienna; Museo degli Argenti, Florence; etc.) that repeat the central panel of Roger van der Weyden's *St John* triptych. When the relationship is harder to trace, a source of inspiration can generally be adduced; for instance, the *Annunciation* and the *Adoration* in the Musée des Gobelins have affinities with Vrancke van der Stocken, while the tender yet regal *Virgin in Glory* (dated 1489) in the Louvre recalls the work of the Maître des Feuillages en Broderie.

The cornice and subdivisions into triptychs framing the various episodes alone indicate an inspiration taken from pictorial or plastic works which were not intended to have any connection with weaving. Finally this method of narration was employed commonly even in cartoons, as can be seen in the famous *'tapis d'or'* at the end of the century (so called on account of the abundant use of gold thread). The narrative tension which is so characteristic of the Tournai tapestries is suddenly relaxed and replaced by an ordered rhythmical composition calculated to reveal the quality of the woven material, as well as the subtle imagery.

The *Stories of the Virgin* in the Spanish collections and the *Apotheosis of Charles VIII*—recently restored to its original vast size in the Metropolitan Museum in New York—are true and genuine 'woven' altarpieces. The scenes, ideally connected by the pious bonds of the concordance to the *Bible of the Poor* and the *Mirror of Human Salvation,* are materially divided by small arches and columns in imitation of the wooden engraved and gilded cornices of church altarpieces. Later, in the 16th century, these visible divisions disappeared, and tapestries were framed in figured borders of flowers and fruit, while the composition retained the earlier clear rhythm, with its balance and feeling of space. An ideal of lightness and elegance, full of tender and noble composure, it eschews all adventurous or romantic tendencies. It seems as if the tapestry now aimed at depicting not life so much as devout contemplation, moral allegory and edifying fables.

These fables dealt with happenings in the past which, it was supposed, could never be repeated. This did not mean that the tapestry weavers rejected their own contemporary world, or the society which commissioned their work. On the contrary, it was a society which was always changing; and the art of the tapestry, reflecting the new tastes, began a transformation from being 'a woven wall' into a fabric which, according to the prevailing fashion, was more decorative than utilitarian.

The creator of the Brussels style of weaving, in the first quarter of the 16th century—a period dubbed the 'Belle Epoque'—is generally thought to be Jan van Roome, who did the rough sketch for the *Communion of Herkenbald* in the Musées Royaux d'Art et d'Histoire in Brussels.

The official position of Jan van Roome, who was court painter to Margaret of Austria, sister of the Emperor Charles V, might be described as 'leader of tapestry style', although he had plenty of highly qualified contemporary craftsmen.

We know for instance of Knoest, who signed the *Finding of the Cross,* now in the Musées Royaux d'Art et d'Histoire at Brussels, and the variously identified 'Philiep' whose name is woven into the *Descent from the Cross* in the same collection, a work closely related to the other *Descent* in the Palazzo Reale, Naples. In both works Italian knowledge and influence is superimposed on Flemish tradition, revealing generally the full extent of contemporary civilisation across Europe.

The story of the Brussels looms, however, has still not been fully traced. Some outstanding tapestries, generally attributed to itinerant weavers in the Loire valley, have been related to Brussels. But we have not yet enough knowledge either to confirm or to deny this contention.

The origin, as well as the date, of some series remained for a long time mysterious. The theory that they were done by itinerant weavers from central France has been widely held. Among these are the six celebrated tapestries of the *Dame à la Licorne* in the Musée de Cluny, with the arms of the La Viste family. This decorative work of exceptional quality reflects an heraldic and courtly ideal, more abstract than real, subscribed to more as a beautiful myth than history. There are obvious affinities with certain Flemish examples, as much in the weave as in the design. A credible parallel can be drawn connecting a particular figure in the *Dame à la Licorne* series with certain others in the *Story of Perseus* (private collection), and with the *Illustrious Women* in a series woven between 1480 and 1482 bearing the arms of Cardinal Ferry de Clugny (fragment in the Museum of Fine Arts, Boston). However, the *Dame à la Licorne* was dated later (about 1509–1513) by most scholars and incidentally seemed somewhat archaic. Recently a comparison of the background of the *Dame à la Licorne* tapestries with the tapestry in Berne bearing the coat-of-arms of Philip the Good of Burgundy, which was certainly woven in Brussels, has revealed striking similarities; and historical research has shown that the set in the Musée de Cluny in Paris was woven for Jean La Viste before 1500, probably in 1480–1490. Indeed the very existence of the itinerant weavers seems now to be questionable.

The Brussels origin of the *Dame à la Licorne*

throws a new light on the origin of many other celebrated tapestries, for instance the *Unicorn Hunt,* which once belonged to Anne of Brittany and is now in the Metropolitan Museum, New York. The same can be said of the *Scenes from Pastoral Life,* in the Musée des Gobelins and the Metropolitan Museum, New York, of the *Feudal Life* in the Musée de Cluny, and of the *Triumphs of Petrarch* in the Kunsthistorisches Museum in Vienna.

FLANDERS AND ITALY

Flanders under the Hapsburgs

In Brussels even more tapestries were produced, to satisfy the ever-increasing commissions. Because high-warp technique had for some time been too slow, it was supplanted by the horizontal loom (low-warp) which, by the use of pedals for working the threads of the warp, accelerated the process and simplified access to the cartoons placed below the loom. The cartoons belonged to the weaver, who could alter tham as he wished, lend them to colleagues or sell them. Two, three or four copies were usually made of each tapestry.

Among well-established workshops were those of Pieter van Aelst and Pieter Pannemaker. The former was accredited to Pope Leo X and the three generations of reigning princes, Maximilian of Austria, Philip the Handsome and the Emperor Charles V. He produced a number of famous series—the *Passion* in the cathedral of Trento and in the Spanish national collection (1507), the *History of David* in the castle of Sigmaringen and, most famous of all, the *Acts of the Apostles* from the Raphael cartoons. Pieter Pannemaker's workshop is credited with the *History of David,* now in the Musée de Cluny, with the tapestry, thought to have been made for the throne of the Emperor Charles V, in the Spanish collection, and, less definitely, with the admirable *Last Supper* in the Museo d'Arte Sacra at Camaiore (1516).

The great success of the Brussels tapestries throughout Europe was partly due to contemporary conditions. In 1519 the Emperor Charles V inherited the lands of Burgundy, Austria, Castille and Aragon, becoming thereby ruler of the greatest empire in the world. Vast riches flowed into a court which dominated Europe and set social canons, at once luxurious and dignified, for the Western world. Princes, dignitaries of the Church and the aristocracy all vied with one another to own the precious narrative tapestries of Flanders. Faced with this demand, designs in the style of Jan van Roome's *hortus conclusus,* charming and delightful though they were, became out of date.

The Influence of Italy

A new style came from Italy, powerfully influenced by Raphael's cartoons for the *Acts of the Apostles.* Italy at this time was not yet an important centre for weaving. Itinerant weavers passed through Siena, Venice, Rome, Correggio and Ferrara, but their output had been small, no more than a few local commissions. There were of course a few outstanding exceptions—the *Passion* in the Museo di S. Marco in Venice, which is attributed to the designs of Zanino di Pietro or Nicolò di Pietro (*c.* 1420–1430), a powerful and expressive work, but unique of its kind. Then there is the *Descent from the Cross,* in the Lenbach Collection and the Cleveland Museum of Art, which was undoubtedly woven in Ferrara from cartoons by Cosimo Tura, and the elegant classical *Annunciation,* bearing the Gonzaga arms, now in the Art Institute of Chicago. These are all fine examples of 15th-century weaving.

A particularly valuable series is *The Months* in the Castello Sforzesco, Milan, woven from designs attributed to Bramantino. This is the first series in which the Renaissance canons of space and perspective were methodically incorporated in tapestries, and with singular effect. But this was an isolated example. When Pope Leo X commissioned Raphael to design the tapestries for the Sistine chapel, he knew that the cartoons should be sent for weaving to van Aelst's workshop in Brussels.

Raphael's influence on the art of tapestry has been exhaustively discussed. It is important to realise that Raphael did not intend merely to transfer his pictorial art onto the loom. His aim was different—to introduce both spiritual and figurative symbols in a balanced and rational composition.

The influence his cartoons had on the Brussels craftsmen was overwhelming. He gave the death blow to the concept of the 'woven wall', although the monumental function of the tapestry was preserved. Henceforth decoration had to conform to architectural structure and narrative to the intellectual demands of the cartoon.

The arrival in Italy of the tapestries provoked various reactions—mainly, according to Michiel and Vasari, astonishment above all at the technical quality of the weaving, and also at the exactness with which the tapestry followed the original painting. This appreciation each had for the other did not necessarily involve a full understanding, but the weaving of the *Acts* (1515–1519) marked the beginning of a long series of exchanges between the northern weavers and Italian painters.

The next works were the lost *Putti at Play,* commissioned at Brussels by Leo X after cartoons by Giovanni da Udine, the *Grottesche,* also designed by Giovanni da Udine for Leo X (and also lost), the *Life of Christ* by van Aelst from cartoons by the school of Raphael (Vatican), a request to Giulio Romano for cartoons for the *History of Scipio,* from which the first tapestry was woven in the studio of Marc Crétif for Francis I of France (1531), and the execution in Brussels of the *Last Supper* by Leonardo da Vinci, and offered by Francis I to Pope Clement VII (Vatican).

THE FLEMISH ROMANISTS

Italian and Flemish relations in the domain of tapestry were further advanced with the reforms inaugurated by Flemish painters who had worked in Italy—such well known artists as Bernard van

1. Cloth of St Gereon (fragment). Cologne. 11th century.
Musée des Tissus, Lyon.

2. *Apocalypse of St John. The Fifth Angel.* Last quarter of the 14th century. Musée des Tapisseries, Angers.

3. *Apocalypse of St John. St Michael and the Devil.* Paris. Last quarter of the 14th century. Musée des Tapisseries, Angers.

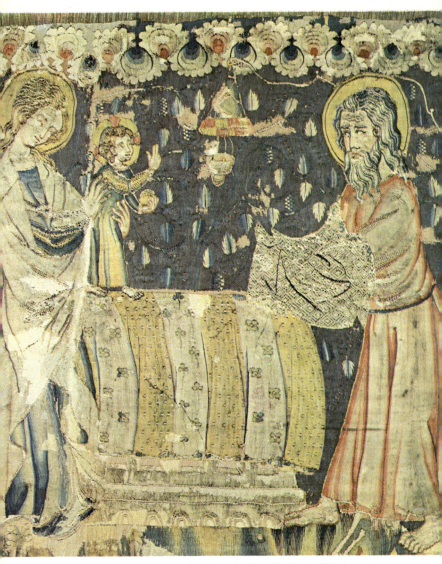

4. *The Presentation in the Temple* (detail). Paris. Third quarter
of the 14th century. Musées Royaux d'Art et d'Histoire, Brussels.

5. *History of St Piat and St Eleuthère. St Eleuthère raising the Tribune's Daughter from the Dead.* Arras. 1402. Tournai cathedral.

6. *The Offering of the Heart.* Arras. Beginning of the 15th century. Musée des Arts Décoratifs, Paris.

7. *Story of Alexander the Great.* Episode in a battle (detail).
Tournai. 1459. Doria Pamphili Collection, Rome.

8. *The Legend of Herkenbald* (detail). *Trajan's Justice*.
Tournai. Before 1461. Historisches Museum, Berne.

9. *The Ball of the Savages* (detail). *c.* mid 15th centur
Musée des Arts Décoratifs, Saumu

10. Floral Tapestry with the arms of Philip the Good. Brussels.
1466. Historisches Museum, Berne.

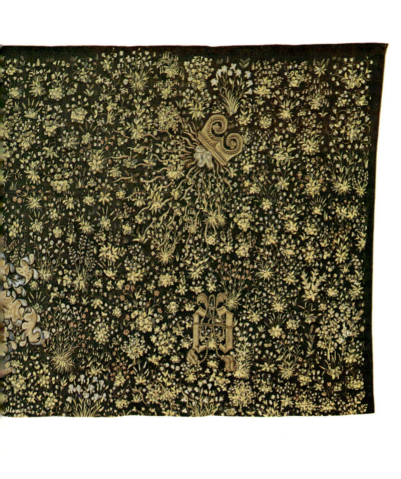

11. *Wild Man with the Unicorn*. The upper Rhine. First quarter
of the 15th century. Museum of Fine Arts, Boston.

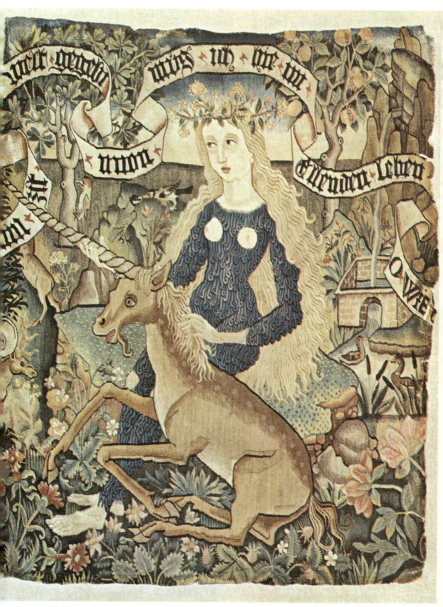

12. *Wild Woman with the Unicorn*. The upper Rhine. Last quarter of the 15th century. Historisches Museum, Basel.

13. *The Virgin in Glory*. Brussels. 1489. Louvre, Paris.

14. *The Communion of Herkenbald*. Brussels. 15
Musées Royaux d'Art et d'Histoire, Brusse

15. *The Last Supper* (detail). Brussels. 1516. Museo d'Arte Sacra, Camaiore.

Orley (who superintended the weaving of the *Acts of the Apostles* at Brussels), Michiel Coxcie, Pieter Coecke van Aelst and Jan Vermeyen. This change in taste was gradual and many of the older features still appeared—as in the fine *Hunts of Maximilian of Austria* by Bernard van Orley. The adoption of the Renaissance perspective, of vision in depth, is counterbalanced by an artificial composition, permitting the full covering of the wall usually by landscapes, in the background of the tapestry. The aim was clearly to retain the old weaving practices, which appeared indigenous to the tapestry, while incorporating the fresh elements.

Contemporary and traditional tastes combined are also evident in the work of Pieter Coecke; in the *History of St Paul* (Vienna) and, particularly, in the *Seven Deadly Sins* (Madrid). The cartoons of Michiel Coxcie are more in the manner of Raphael. The first tapestry woven from his *Story of Genesis* is in the Wawel Castle Museum, Krakow, although here the craftsman has striven too hard for an expression which he has not fully understood.

The full effects of the new manner were not immediately evident. Jan Vermeyen, who designed the formal *Conquest of Tunis* commissioned by the Emperor Charles V (1554), turned to Mannerist themes in his *Vertumnus and Pomona*. He used designs after the 'pergola school' that followed Giulio Romano, which were also being woven at Brussels, in the studio of Willem Pannemaker at the same time as *Putti at Play* (Madrid).

Willem Pannemaker, the son of Pieter, was one of

the most important weavers then working in Brussels. Supplying the courts of the Emperors Charles V and Philip II, he produced some well known series, such as the *Conquest of Tunis,* the *Seven Deadly Sins,* a copy of van Orley's *History of Jacob* (Uffizi), the *Apocalypse* (Madrid), the *Months of Luke* (possibly from cartoons by Lucas van Nevele) and the marvellous *Verdure with large foliage* bearing the arms of the Emperor Charles V (Vienna).

After 1528 the attribution of the various series to different workshops becomes easier. This was the year in which the municipality of Brussels instructed the various workshops to use two trademarks, one for the city (a red shield between two B's, initials of Brussels and Brabant) and a personal one. These trademarks are not all identifiable, although those of the major weavers are known. In addition to the Pannemakers were Willem de Kempeneere, who wove the earliest known series of the *History of Jacob,* which belonged to Cardinal Campeggi of Bologna (Musées Royaux d'Art et d'Histoire, Brussels); the Leyniers, weavers of the first tapestry of the *Story of Genesis* and the *History of Romulus and Remus*; and Frans Guebels, whose signature is on the *Seven Virtues,* the *Months* (Vienna) and the *Triumph of the Gods* in the Mobilier National of Paris, as well as many other tapestries.

16th-CENTURY ITALIAN TAPESTRIES

Ferrara

In various Italian centres the art of the tapestry had an unforeseen success in the middle of the 16th century. It may seem strange that workshops should have been opened in Italy at the moment when tapestries in the Italian style could be bought in Flanders, where they were even designed by Italian artists. In fact it was this stylistic uniformity which favoured the opening of the new workshops. The Prince who commissioned tapestries from Flanders could be certain of finding master-weavers to reproduce the cartoons of local painters; the latter had already had some experience in executing designs for tapestries.

The first workshop was opened in Ferrara by Ercole II d'Este. He employed in his service as tapestry repairers the Flemings Jan and Nicolaus Carcher (or Karcher). In 1536 he enlisted eight other northern craftsmen, among them Jan Rost. They immediately set to work. All this can be deduced from the ducal accounts, which include payments for cartoons in this year to Battista Dossi, brother of the more famous Dosso Dossi. Among the first subjects referred to is the *History of Hercules,* a mythological paean to the reigning Duke. In 1545 payments are mentioned for cartoons of Ovid's *Metamorphoses.* His last series, which is partially preserved (Louvre and private collections), bears the trademark of Jan Carcher, the date being 1545 and the inscription *'Factum Ferrariae'*. The subjects with their learned and mythological allusions were certainly inspired by a man of letters. This literary inspiration did not, however, limit the designer's fantasy; indeed it stimulated it, encouraging him to handle the theme imaginatively. And the theme was repeated in every tapestry, in the nymph-like trees, living trunks, as it were, supporting an architecture of branches frozen into a mysterious immobility. Such were the 'poetic' (using this word in its 16th-century sense) developments in evocative and allegorical painting. Though full of fantasy, the *History of St George and St Maurelius* (1552–1553), which are now in Ferrara cathedral, exhale a different and less rarified atmosphere.

Duke Ercole died in 1559. The production of tapestries, of which he had been the patron, declined under his successor Alfonso, who did not share his enthusiasm for the art. The weaving of the *Story of the Virgin,* from designs by Arcimboldo for Como cathedral was continued. This was the last documented series from the Ferrara workshops, of which, after 1582, nothing more is known.

Mantua

The life-span of the Gonzaga workshops at Mantua was even briefer; they depended on the peregrinations of Nicolaus Carcher who was 'lent' by the Estes to the Gonzagas, and lived there from 1539 to 1541. He suddenly left for Florence, and only returned in

1555 to Mantua, where he died in 1562. Irregular production makes the attribution of any important series to Mantua more difficult than to Ferrara. Such series were the *History of Moses* and *Putti at Play* in Milan cathedral, *Putti at Play* in the Museo Poldi Pezzoli, Milan, and in the Gulbenkian Foundation, Lisbon. *Putti at Play,* dignified with the coat-of-arms of Cardinal Ercole Gonzaga, was certainly designed by Giulio Romano; he used the motif of the pergola and the children playing around it as a means of giving unity and decoration to his compositions. Tapestry seemed to have again become a 'woven wall', but this time a Mannerist 'wall', involving a clever inter-penetration of real and imaginary space, and intro-ducing a subtle element of mythological fantasy. The weave is so similar to that of the *Metamorphoses* that it is more reasonable to attribute it to Ferrara than Mantua.

The difference may be seen by comparing this series with the *Putti at Play* and the *History of Moses*. In the latter the colouring is flamboyant and the border garlands drawn from nature. The architectural effects are formal, but the whole is permeated with a curious fantasy which relates it to Ferrara. However, this is a question which perhaps we shall never be able to answer.

Florence and Mannerism

Giorgio Vasari relates that Cosimo I de' Medici wished to establish tapestry workshops in Florence because, in a city so rich in arts and crafts, this was the only one missing. His intention was to include all the arts and sciences, the purely aesthetic as well as the educative. There were other reasons no doubt, commercial and financial, reflected in the contracts he drew up on 20th October 1546 with the weavers Jan Rost and Nicolaus Carcher. The contracts stipulate that these master craftsmen shall also instruct local workers, that the weavers shall 'take an interest in design', and that they must undertake, as Riccio writes, 'to be original'. This last stipulation was fully observed. The first series woven was the *History of Joseph* for the Sala dei Dugento in the Palazzo Vecchio (1546–1553). Pontormo was commissioned for the designs but, according to Vasari, 'these pleased neither the Duke nor the weavers'; for this reason Bronzino was entrusted with the main designs. Confronted with the task of giving the tapestry a monumental quality in keeping with the delicacy of the weave, he broke up the groups of figures, giving them different proportions and ingeniously covering the entire surface of the tapestry with distinctive shapes and colours. In this novel or, as Vasari terms it, 'strange' manner, the harmonious idealised composition of Raphael's *Acts* was surpassed, and a new graphic and decorative style emerged, of great sensual as well as cerebral intensity. Bronzino later adopted this manner for his allegorical *portieres* (*Flora, Justice*), culminating in his heraldic cryptogram, the *Apotheosis of the House of Medici* (Uffizi Gallery, Florence).

The problem of relating painting to tapestry, which

Bronzino resolved by the sheer virtuosity of his composition, was investigated further by Francesco Salviati. He regarded the tapestry as a unique form of pictorial expression, almost a rival of painting, but possessing its own special expression. Particularly in the small religious tapestries (*Ecce Homo,* the *Resurrection* and the *Descent from the Cross*) Salviati, while retaining a feeling of high culture and of intellectual research, was searching for a dramatic, pathetic or grotesque meaning, which, in the woven version, takes on a particular force of its own. Equally elegant is the series designed by Francesco Ubertini, who was known as Bachiacca. In the *Grotesques* the woven background seems at first a decorative caprice; but soon it is apparent that it is the fruit of much thought, as is the basis of the *Months* (1552–1553) in the Uffizi Gallery, Florence.

The contribution of the Florentine Mannerists to the art of tapestry was coherent and aesthetic, employing valuable cloth and beautiful weaving methods. This was no vulgar display of luxury but a serious attempt to interpret the subtleties and singularities of the designer and the meaning of the cartoons. They were linked closely to an aesthetic idea and were representative of a society whose interests were pre-eminently intellectual.

In 1557 the Fleming, Jan van der Straet, called Stradanus, was appointed designer to the Medicean tapestry works. Vasari, who supervised, evolved a composite plan for the tapestries in the Palazzo Vecchio, eulogising either directly or in mythological form the stories and virtues of the House of Medici.

He supervised themes and possibly some of the compositions; the designs were executed by Stradanus, with the characteristic speed of the Flemish cartoonists. The woven work on the other hand no longer possessed the old elegance, although the high technical level was retained. Few of the tapestries known to us from documents have survived. In the *Florentine Chronicles* (Accademia, Uffizi, Palazzo Davanzati, Biblioteca Laurenziana, Florence) there is a mixture of courtliness and erudition typical of the whole production in the Palazzo Vecchio after Vasari's appointment. The brilliance of Stradanus lies in his narrative power and realism, well exemplified in the *Hunt* series for the Medici villa of Poggio a Cajano. Though the themes are Flemish, they are handled with the plastic and dramatic skill of the Florentines. The series was begun in 1567. Stradanus left Florence in 1576, and the *Hunt* series was completed from designs by the new cartoonist of the Medici workshop, Alessandro Allori.

During his long and arduous career as a cartoonist, Allori continued the traditions of the Florentine workshop, not only as interpreted recently by Stradanus, but also with the older and better known methods of Bronzino. The two are far from similar, but Allori succeeded in combining them, endowing them with academic dignity. To list all the tapestries woven from his designs by Florentine weavers (under the direction successively of Giovanni Sconditi, Benedetto Squilli and Guasparri Papini) would take too long. We will confine ourselves to mentioning the panels for the ducal houses, and the commissions for 'foreigners'—the *Stories of the Virgin* in the church of Sta Maria Maggiore at Bergamo, the *Prefiguration of the Holy Sacraments* in Como cathedral, and many others.

THE LATE 16TH CENTURY IN BRUSSELS AND ELSEWHERE

Wars and religious struggles were responsible for a certain thematic and technical deficiency in tapestry production. At this time landscapes with animals and the hunting series were extremely popular. In these the horizontal line is emphasised, and the densely crowded figures cover the entire tapestry; they are depicted in autumnal tints, faded greens, browns and yellows. This is not great art, but it has decorative value, because the tapestries are eminently suited for the house, possessing again their traditional high viewpoint and the old protective function as woven screens. They are great banks of greenery, set in motion not by the clashing of Gothic warriors, but by gentle zephyrs, suitable for an increasingly bourgeois society.

A celebrative series of high quality, such as the *Feasts of the Valois* (Uffizi, Florence), woven about 1582–1585 after designs by Antoine Caron from cartoons by Lucas de Heere, seemed at that time unique. Sumptuous, of refined colouring in the Mannerist style, with portraits taken from life of great psychological insight, the series stands out among Brussels tapestries, and it is not certain whether it was woven at Brussels or at Antwerp. That the situation in Flanders was difficult for the weavers is proved by the mass emigration of those who were Protestant—for the benefit of other nations, especially Germany. Tapestry works were established in many cities—Stuttgart (where Jakob de Carmes worked), Kassel, Frankenthal, Cologne, Heidelberg, Lüneburg, Torgau, Leipzig (where the famous *Allegory of the Reformation* was woven), Wesel, Wiemar, Dresden and Hamburg. Their output was remarkable for its variety of techniques and styles, although with a common basis of expression. This last can be explained by the common origin of the Flemish weavers, and the former by their continual movement from one place to another as working conditions required. No workshop was pre-eminent, and production in one place never continued for long. A close examination of these vicissitudes for each individual work of art would be outside the scope of this book. Flemish weavers found asylum also in Denmark, Sweden and Holland, where a workshop was established by Frans Spierinck in 1591.

The *History of Diana* (Knole, Kent), the *History of Orlando Furioso* (Museo Poldi Pezzoli, Milan; County Museum, Los Angeles) and the *History of Scipio* sufficiently illustrate the great interpretative qualities of this weaver, a native of Brussels, who worked in Antwerp before moving to Delft. The exiled weavers, who gave their techniques and, perhaps more important, a taste for tapestry to all Europe, did not all come from Brussels; some were from lesser centres.

Oudenaarde, Enghien, Grammont, Antwerp and Bruges all enjoyed a certain reputation.

It is difficult to name the designers of the tapestries woven in Flanders during the late 16th and early 17th centuries, especially those of the landscapes and hunting scenes. And it is seldom possible to relate them to well known designers of the period; when this has been done, it was generally through prints. For example, the medallions in the borders of several series from Brussels (the *History of Hercules, c.* 1570, in the Musées Royaux d'Art et d'Histoire, Brussels; the *History of Troy,* private collection, Venice) were inspired by subjects deriving from Pieter Bruegel the Elder, and the Antwerp series of the *Labours of Hercules* from compositions of Floris engraved by M. du Bos. It seems that painters could no longer impose their own choice, which they left to the weavers.

RUBENS TAPESTRIES

The art of tapestry was suddenly changed by the unexpected advent of Rubens, who introduced many important modifications. One technical alteration was due to the fact that he made his own coloured designs (enlarged into cartoons by pupils) in oils, not tempera, as was customary in the past. This presented the weavers with difficult problems (how were they to reproduce in the weave transparent and diaphanous elements and the sophisticated lighting effects?) which were only partly solved by cross-hatching with different colours. But the most important change was in the new composition and expression.

If we must find a suitable name for this style, it is 'Baroque', at least in the sense that the woven background became an artificial stage set only just containing the gigantic figures of gods and heroes, vices and virtues, densely massed and participating in certain specific actions. Compared with the decorative detail, the backgrounds counted for little. All subsidiary figures are eliminated from the canvas; the protagonists must belong figuratively to the powerful social world to which Rubens belonged.

The *History of Decius Mus* was already, in 1617, on the looms of Jan Raes and Frans van den Hecke. The *History of Constantine* (1623–1624), the first tapestry of which was woven not in Brussels but in Paris, was commissioned by Louis XIII of France. Compared with other series designed by Rubens, its composition has a static quality, supposedly linked to the influence of classic models. The hypothesis is probably sound, although adherence to the antique forms did not hamper the artist's original genius. In the *Battle of the Milvian Bridge* the tangled group of knights and their horses plunging headlong into the river mingling with the ruined arches of the bridge is a masterpiece of Baroque boldness.

The first cartoons were seen in a preview in Paris by 'almost all those employed by the King in public works', among them Peiresc, who told Rubens that 'they all had to confess that these were the work of a great man, of the noblest genius . . . Particularly admired on the ruined bridge were the two figures hanging by their hands, one of which, the wounded man hanging by one hand, seems to me perfect and inimitable (although certain experts talk of artistic deficiencies in the lower part of the thigh), while the other man, suspended by two hands, was the object of general admiration.' The criticisms of the French courtiers were, taken all in all, largely academic, and they ignored the purpose and hanging of the cartoon. The distorted proportions were intentional, to give animation to the scene.

In 1627–1628 Jan Raes wove the first tapestry of the *Triumph of the Eucharist,* commissioned by the Archduchess Isabella for the Monasterio de las Descalzas Reales in Madrid, where it still is. The theme was based on the figurative tradition of 'triumphs'; but even these acquire in Rubens' hands new and varied implications. The allegory is duly expressed, but it is the human vitality which predominates, seeming even to overflow the borders, which have now become an integral part of the main composition. This was the end of those ornate flower borders, with mythological and grotesque animals, which had recently been vying with the central design. Instead the columns, like architectural frames, support undulating draperies, framing the eucharistic processions. Nothing was to distract or divert the attention from the main theme. The same energy is seen in the *Achilles* series, started by Rubens and completed by Jakob Jordaens (Museum of Fine Arts, Boston; Palazzi Reali, Turin and Carignano; and numerous other collections).

Skill in relating episodes and narration reappeared in the works of the designer Jakob Jordaens. Though in the tradition of Rubens, he was somewhat freer in treatment. He left many series: the *Ulysses* (Palazzo Reale, Turin; Quirinale, Rome; weaver, G. van der Strecken); the *History of Alexander*; the *History of Charlemagne* (Quirinale, Rome; weavers, J. Cordys and M. Roelants); *Country Life* (Vienna; weaver, C. van der Bruggen); *Great Horses* (Vienna; weavers, H. Reydams and E. Leyniers); the *Proverbs* (Vienna; weaver, J. Cordys; and the Diocesan Museum, Tarragona). The same motif was repeated in several series, with a facility of adaptation which showed that Jordaens aimed principally at pleasant decorative effects. In the *Months,* from cartoons by van den Hoecke, the decorative character can always be seen in the lively pictorial design, which shows the influence of the French tapestry in Brussels.

Yet Flemish weavers were still flourishing. Work went on in Antwerp as well as Brussels (*Dido and Aeneas* by Wauters from cartoons by Romanelli), and in Oudenaarde (*Calvary* in the church of Sta Maria Maggiore at Bergamo; weaver, Jan Regelbrugghe). The Brussels workshops produced tapestries of the highest quality; but from the middle of the 17th century they encountered difficulties. The House of Austria, on which Flanders depended politically, supported the industry with large orders; occasionally there were clients such as Charles Emanuel II of Savoy who, over a period of ten years, ordered hundreds of tapestries for the new royal palace in Turin. But the markets in France, Holland, England and Italy were more difficult, for workshops were being opened there in increasing quantities, and competition became fiercer.

They attempted a revival, taking advantage of the fashion for 'Tenières' genre tapestries based on the pictures of Teniers and other painters of his school, which had an enormous success. But this very success was a disadvantage, because their work was immediately copied everywhere.

THE GOLDEN AGE OF FRENCH TAPESTRIES

The Establishment of Tapestry Works in Paris

After the short-lived venture of Fontainebleau where Francis I established a court workshop to weave copies of frescoes in the Galerie des Reformés by Primaticcio and Rosso (the series is now in the Kunsthistorisches Museum, Vienna) there was a half-hearted attempt in the 16th century to establish a workshop in Paris. The first of any importance was established in 1601 by two Flemings, Marc de Comans and François de La Planche (van den Planken), to whom Henry IV accorded especial privileges.

Here the *Artemis* series was woven and often copied (Mobilier National, Paris: Institute of Art, Minneapolis: Palazzo Chiablese, Palazzo Reale and

Palazzo Madama, Turin). Designed by Caron in honour of Catherine de Médicis, it was later adapted by Lerambert in honour of Marie de Médicis. The result was one of the most outstanding series of this type ever woven. The story of the mythical queen of Caria, inconsolable widow of Mausolus and wise tutoress of the young heir to the throne, had a very special topical association in France for the Queen Mother.

The identification of legendary with historical personalities is here ingeniously enacted. From its deliberate mannerism, the style may be considered archaic, in view of the date of its weaving; but the attempt at expressing historical and political significance is perfectly contemporary, and it was copied and recopied in France throughout the 17th century.

François de La Planche died in 1627, and Marc de Comans retired in 1628. Their sons continued the workshop until 1633. Raphael de La Planche moved to the Faubourg St Germain, whilst the de Comans remained in their old premises in the Faubourg St Marcel (at one time the home of a Paris family of dyers, the Gobelins). Meanwhile Maurice Dubourg and Girard Laurent had set up looms in the Grande Galerie du Louvre. All these workshops employed the Paris trademark (a 'P' with the fleur-de-lys of France) and the same cartoons. There is plenty of documentary evidence about the sharing of cartoons for the series inspired and painted by Simon Vouet (the *Rinaldo and Armida*, the *Loves of the Gods* and the Old Testament scenes). While retaining the traditional qualities of French tapestry, innovations were

16. *Descent from the Cross*. Brussels. First quarter of the 16th century. Milan cathedral.

17. *Descent from the Cross* (detail). Brussels. First quarter
of the 16th century. Milan cathedral.

18. *Esther and Ahasuerus.* Brussels. First quarter of the 16th century. Museo Poldi Pezzoli, Milan.

19. *La Dame à la Licorne. The Unicorn and the Mirror.*
Brussels. *c.* 1480-1490. Musée de Cluny, Paris.

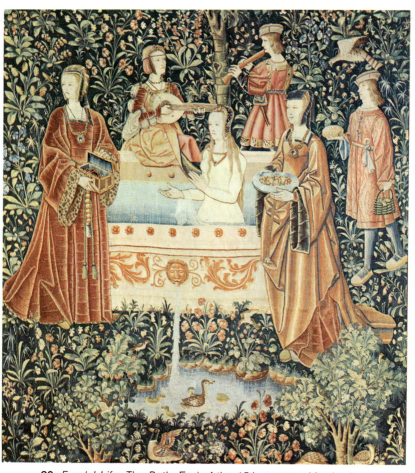

20. *Feudal Life. The Bath*. End of the 15th century. Musée de Cluny, Paris.

21. *The Triumphs of Petrarch. The Triumph of Time over Fame* (detail). Flemish. End of the 15th century. Kunsthistorisches Museum, Vienna.

22. *The Triumphs of Petrarch. The Triumph of Death over Chastity* (detail showing Pandora). Flemish. End of 15th century. Kunsthistorisches Museum, Vienna.

pandora

23. *Christ's Passion. The Last Supper.* Venice. *c.* 1420-1430. S. Marco, Venice.

24. *Christ's Passion. Christ before Pilate.* Venice. *c.* 1420-1430.
S. Marco, Venice.

26. *The Acts of the Apostles. The Miraculous Draught of Fishes. c.* 1540. Palazzo Ducale, Mantua.

27. *The Acts of the Apostles. St Peter healing the Cripple.*
Brussels. *c.* 1540. Palazzo Ducale, Mantua.

28. *Story of Genesis. The Expulsion of Adam and Eve from the Garden of Eden.* Brussels. Mid 16th century. Accademia, Florence.

29. *The Battle of Pavia. The Cavalry Charge.* Brussels.
c. 1530. Museo di Capodimonte, Naples.

Within the tapestry, on a banner:

GEORGIVS·XPI·MILES·
DRACONEM·INTERFICIT·
·REGISQ·FILIAM·
·A·MORTE·LIBERAT·

30. *The History of St George and St Maurelius. St George Slays the Dragon.* Ferrara? 1552-1553. Ferrara cathedral.

31. *Putti at Play. The Arbour.* Ferrara. *c.* 1540-1545. Museo Poldi Pezzoli, Milan.

32. *The History of Moses. The Brazen Serpent.* After 1550?
Milan cathedral.

33. *The History of Joseph. Joseph repulsing Potiphar's Wife.*
Florence. 1549. Palazzo Vecchio, Florence.

34. *Ecce Homo*. Florence. 1549. Uffizi Gallery, Florence.

35. *The Months. June and July* (detail of the *June Harvest*
Florence. 1553. Uffizi Gallery, Florence

36. *The Hunts. Hunting the Wild Cat.* Florence. 1577. Palazzo Vecchio, Florence.

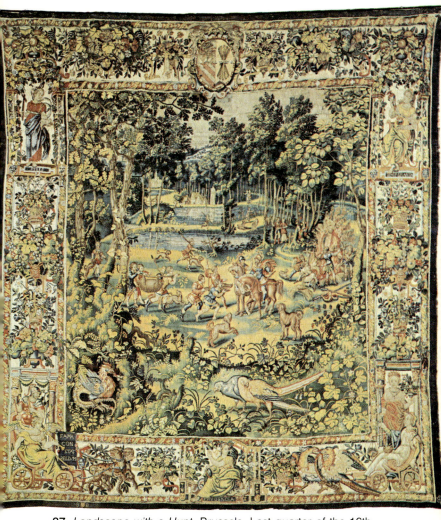

37. *Landscape with a Hunt.* Brussels. Last quarter of the 16th century. Museo Civico, Turin.

38. *The History of Orlando Furioso* (detail). Delft. Early 17th century. Museo Poldi Pezzoli, Milan.

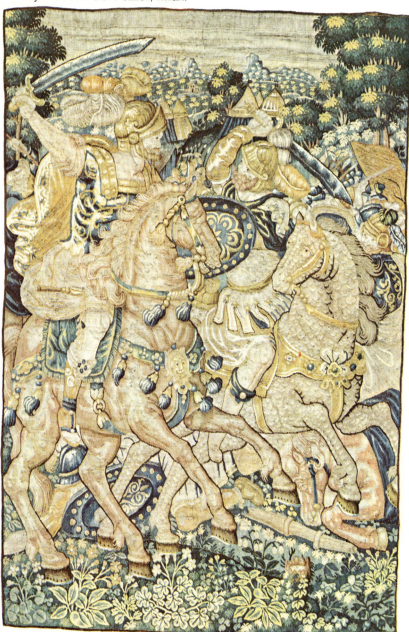

39. *The History of Troy.* Oudenaarde. Late 16th century. Private Collection. Venice.

40. *Altarpiece of the Doge Marino Grimani*. Florence. 1595.
S. Marco, Venice.

41. *The Triumph of the Eucharist. The Miraculo[us]*
Fall of Manna (detail). Brussels. Mid 17th centur[y]
Palazzo Reale, Tur[in]

42. *The History of Achilles and the Centaur Chiron.* Brussels.
Mid 17th century. Palazzo Reale, Turin.

43. *The History of Aurelian and Zenobia. Zenobia as a Prisoner.* Brussels. End of the 17th century. Musées Royaux d'Art et d'Histoire, Brussels.

GRAMMATICA·
HÆC CVPIENTI·
DISCERE·PRIMA·EST·

44. *The Liberal Arts. The Grammar Lesson*. Bruges. *c.* 1665. Castello Sforzesco, Milan.

45. *The History of Artemisia*. Paris. *c.* 1625. Mobilier National, Paris.

46. *The History of Diana. Diana refusing to marry Otus.* Paris. *c.* 1625. Palazzo Reale, Turin.

introduced, as were later to be seen in the royal workshops of the Gobelins.

The Gobelins and Absolute Monarchy

In 1662, by order of Louis XIV, the minister Colbert acquired the land and buildings in the Faubourg St Marcel, already partly occupied by the workshop of the de Comans. All the Paris workshops were moved to this site, and in 1667 the Manufacture Royale des Meubles de la Couronne was founded by letters patent. This was also known as the Gobelins, where engravers, furniture-makers and goldsmiths as well as weavers worked until 1694. The establishment was run on the strictest lines by the State Superintendent, while the Director (Le Brun was the first) was responsible for the artistic side.

Work started on a copy of the *Acts of the Apostles* by Raphael, and with subjects designed earlier in the tapestry works of Fouquet at Maincy by Le Brun; the latter had been preparing new cartoons for the series of the *Elements* (first woven 1664–1669; Palazzo Pubblico, Siena; Palazzo Pitti, Florence), the *Seasons, Children Gardening,* and the great triad in honour of Louis XIV—the *History of Alexander,* the *Life of the King,* and the *Royal Palaces.*

These three series were set on the loom in quick succession, in respectively 1664, 1665 and 1668, and completed between 1680 and 1681 (Mobilier National, Paris). They all treat broadly of the same theme, the glorification of the king, who is identified with the state. The glorification is achieved, in the *History of*

Alexander, by means of allusions. This indirect approach is significant and clearly reveals the aesthetic programme of the artist. Le Brun combines an articulated and modulated composition, strictly balancing the proportions with an intellectual severity, permitting daring innovations. Flattery of the monarch is more evident in the *Life of the King,* where the schematic development of the horizontal setting and the display of ceremony have the effect of focusing attention on him. The combination of an intellectual concept with scenic effects is typical of the 17th century. The same may be said for architecture and stage scenery. In short, Le Brun felt and expressed the taste of his times as well as the mural and architectural values of tapestry.

The *Life of the King* caused some jealousy among courtiers who thought they should be included in it. Through secret influence the Comte d'Harcourt, known as Cadet la Perle, succeeded in having himself depicted in the *Audience of the Legate* wearing his hat in the presence of the king, a privilege not accorded to him in life (he was content to have it thus in effigy). This detail might have gone down to posterity as a harmless joke, had not Saint-Simon, in his *Memoires,* revealed his vanity. The episode is more important than it seems, for it indicates the social function of the tapestry, a mirror of the world and its customs, as well as the existence of a royal myth. The absolute monarch, not satisfied with announcing his greatness on earth, wished to be regarded as divine, while his courtiers were demi-gods, all living together in the new Olympus at Versailles and the other royal residences. The third series by Le Brun dealt with these *Royal Palaces*.

Places dedicated to the luxury and magnificence of the sovereign, the *'maisons royales'*, are seen in the background. Here the architectural design is not treated in the Rubens manner as an integral part of the action; instead, it is used to mark the separation between the real and the purely evocative, endowing the royal residences with an aura of remote, intangible grandeur.

Le Brun died in 1690 and was succeeded by Pierre Mignard. Considerable difficulties occurred in that year, which led to the closing of the works in 1694. They did not reopen until 1699.

Other Royal Tapestry Workshops

Louis XIV had also established a Manufacture Royale at Beauvais (1664). For the first twenty years of its life it produced works of little merit, but in 1684 the Fleming Philippe Béhagle was appointed intendant. Amongst the series woven under his direction, the *Grotesques,* inspired by Bérain and designed by J. B. Monnoyer, are notable for their entertaining and decorative gaiety, precursors of the 18th-century taste.

The grant of the title 'Manufacture Royale' to the small studios at Aubusson and Felletin during the 17th century was not of much help; production remained small, with landscapes and a few mediocre figurative tapestries.

GERMANY AND ENGLAND

The competition between countries and courts to set up tapestry workshops became increasingly more intense. To obtain able workmen the new studios turned chiefly to the inexhaustible fount of Flanders. Jean van der Biest, who from 1605 to 1613 wove in Munich the *History of Otto von Wittelsbach,* the *Seasons* and the *Months* from designs by Pieter Candido, came from Brussels.

The names of a number of Flemish weavers (such as Philipp de Maecht) are found also at Mortlake in England, where in about 1620 the Crown established a workshop. In 1623 Charles I acquired seven of Raphael's cartoons for the *Acts of the Apostles.* Fine copies were made at Mortlake with elegant new borders, probably designed by Francis Cleyn. The latter certainly designed the cartoons for the series of *Hero and Leander* and of the *Royal Horses,* which was repeated several times. Work stopped during the Civil War; when it restarted, there were great difficulties, and in 1667 the works passed into private hands, only to close completely at the end of the century. The Mortlake weavers migrated to different workshops in Soho, Hatton Garden and other places where they continued their varied and interesting work.

Holland, meanwhile, had been establishing tapestry workshops and had become an important centre of production; and in 1615 Karel van Mander II, already a designer for Spierinck, founded a new tapestry works at Delft.

17TH-CENTURY ITALIAN TAPESTRIES

The Barberini Workshop

The most typical of 17th-century workshops was the private one established in Rome by Cardinal Francesco Barberini, nephew of Pope Urban VIII. The Barberini workshop was directed by a rich and cultivated dilettante and collector of antiques; he was also well versed in inscriptions, history and literature. The work produced here was to the Roman Baroque what the Medici tapestry works had been to the early Florentine Mannerist movement. Its establishment may have been encouraged by Louis XIII's gift to the Cardinal of the first series of the *History of Constantine* (Museum of Art, Philadelphia); this was continued in the Roman workshop, from designs by Pietro da Cortona (1632–1641; Museum of Art, Philadelphia). Though there is a certain resemblance with the Paris series of Rubens, the tapestries designed by Pietro da Cortona differ in their insistent evocation of the ancient world, based on precise literary knowledge. The classical themes are reclad with Baroque sensibility and taste, a flowing eloquence and an even greater arrogance. The choice of subjects is most interesting, ranging from a parallel ideal of Constantine as Christian emperor to 'His most Christian Majesty of France', whose temporal power was exceeded only by the higher spiritual power of the Pontiff—Urban VIII Barberini. In one of the tapestries Constantine is shown killing a lion, the symbol of royalty; this implies that the King of

Heaven will always prevail over the kings of the Earth. The theme of the distinction between heavenly and earthly glory is repeated in another series, the copy (1633–1642; Museo di Palazzo Venezia, Rome) of *Putti at Play* by Giovanni da Udine, then in the Vatican. Romanelli altered the old cartoons, but added an unusual new subject, the *Lion defeated by Bees*. This obvious symbol (bees form part of the Barberini coat of arms) exalted both the House of Pope Urban VIII and the Pontifical political supremacy. The *Mysteries of the Life and Death of Christ* (1643–1646; St John's Cathedral, New York) from designs by Romanelli and Pietro da Cortona was woven for the hall in the Palazzo Barberini, the ceiling of which had been painted by Cortona with the *Triumph of Divine Providence*. The tapestries were to complete a decorative unity and to enforce it by an iconographical link. The allegory on the ceiling, as conceived by Bracciolini, exalted both Divine Providence and the grandeur of the Barberini family. The *Life of Christ* was intended to complete the cycle, celebrating the glory of the Redeemer as well as that of His Vicar, the Roman Pontiff. The theme, in fact, if not exactly profane was far from sacred, with its eulogistic allusions; it is to be read, however, only in connection with the original historical context.

This often happened in Italian tapestries, conceived in terms of complex organic decoration.

When Cardinal Barberini died in 1679 production languished and finally ceased—a fate common to workshops dependent on an individual patron.

The Medici Workshop

The artistic quality of the relatively small production of tapestries from the Barberini workshop was superior to that of the larger Medici workshop in Florence. From the middle of the century the latter seems to have stagnated stylistically. The *Hours* and the *Seasons,* woven between 1630 and 1643, still show considerable talent in the 16th-century style; although not lacking in merit, they do not conform to the taste of the other contemporary workshops. The importation of foreign workers, such as the Fleming van Asselt and the Frenchman Le Févère, did not have the expected results, at least as far as the style of the tapestries woven there was concerned. A certain modernity was attempted by Melissi, especially in his cartoons for the *History of Moses,* repeated several times between 1650 and 1659. A more definite attempt towards the Baroque was made in the third quarter of the century by Giovanni Battista Termini; but he came up against important technical difficulties and abandoned his work, and Florence, to which he only returned in 1703.

18TH-CENTURY FRENCH TAPESTRIES

The Influence of Rococo

The profound change of taste at the turn of the 17th and 18th centuries produced a renaissance, an anti-traditional and anti-academic reaction throughout

Europe. This had such repercussions on tapestry that it caused a complete metamorphosis. 'Caused' is perhaps not the correct term; we can say it accelerated a process already under way. For some time tapestry had ceased to be a 'mainstream art', with an independent life of its own. There were many reasons for this, both historical and practical. The old 'mural' style—in the strictest sense of the word—soon went out of fashion. Decoration of the walls became the main requirement—with wallpaper, carved panelling, leather or other materials.

The celebrative quality in tapestry lasted longer. The 18th century, which was not interested in historical subjects, would have preferred to ignore it entirely and concentrate only on the decorative element, which suited contemporary taste. The woven stuffs had to conform to the stucco, the decorations of walls and ceilings, the pictures, the furniture and its covering. They had to be graceful and witty, in accordance with the new rules of society. When the Gobelins factories reopened they followed these directives. Claude Audran III, who designed the *portières* of the *Gods* (often copied from 1700 onwards) and the grotesques of the *Months* (1708–1710), applied his decorative skill in a charmingly novel way for the *Don Quixote* series. The Knight of the Woeful Countenance, ever in trouble over identities and allusions, is depicted, together with his adventures, the latter recounted from the designs of Charles Antoine Coypel in the central panel, surrounded by real or imaginary adversaries. At least six series were designed, with variations to suit different fashions; they were constantly repeated between 1717 and 1794. Let us examine the second series. The background in imitation damask is framed by borders which give the illusion of a wooden cornice. From this fragile design hang heavy garlands of fruit and flowers, a strange world of monkeys and birds on which flying cherubs look down. Amid tulips and roses, vine tendrils and peaches are pieces of armour and parts of flags, the fond remains of forgotten trophies. In the centre is the 'story', looking like a painting in an ornate frame. The narrative is of such little importance that the surround in the *Don Quixote* series overflows into and encircles the *Fragments from Opera*, the *Scenes from Opera, Tragedy and Comedy* (central subjects by C. A. Coypel), as in the *Loves of the Gods* (central subjects by Boucher; first woven 1758–1762).

The designs of these surrounds had a very practical purpose: their fragmentary structure was an admirable setting for the kaleidoscopic decoration which could thus be altered as the ingenuity of the artist displayed itself. In a Europe bewitched by Rococo this suited the artist well. First came the architects, and in their wake the painters, picture-framers, sculptors and decorators. Tapestry had to follow suit.

The much deprecated 'picturesqueness' of 18th-century decor had therefore a justification; it was the consequence, not the cause, of tapestry's new role.

The Gobelins

The favourite themes and moods of the 18th

century continually recur in the Gobelins works. There is exoticism, with all its nuances, from the fabulous (the *New Indies* by Desportes; first woven 1740–1744) to the picturesque of the *Turkish Embassy* by Parrocel (1731–1737) (woven to commemorate the entry of the Turkish Ambassador, Mehemet Effendi, into Paris in 1721) and the documentaries of *Turkish Scenes* by Charles Amédéé van Loo (first woven 1777–1780). There is the Arcadian 'drawing-room' series of *Daphnis and Chloe* and the mythological gallantry of the *Loves of the Gods,* as well as the melo-dramatic extremes of the *History of Esther* (first woven 1738–1745) and the *History of Jason* (first woven 1750–1754), both from designs by de Troy. There is also the celebrative series of the *Hunts of Louis XV* (1736–1750; Palazzo Pitti, Florence; Château de Compiègne) from designs by Jean Baptiste Oudry, which might be mistaken at first for a sylvan pastoral. The focus is centred on the forests of Compiègne and Fontainebleau, seen as it were in theatrical perspective. The human element is confined to the King and his courtiers whose amiable expressions are characterless, and indistinguishable one from another. The bodies are in keeping with the faces, elegant dummies superbly clad, shimmering in silk and velvet and gold embroidery. A frivolous *divertissement*? Not entirely, for this represented a world which was both imaginary and real, whose weaknesses as well as aspirations it disarmingly displayed.

To adhere to the picturesque was all that 18th-century tapestry could do to escape from the tyranny of exactly reproduced designs; this decision was followed by almost all the workshops, particularly those in France.

Beauvais and Aubusson

The Beauvais school, in which the curious 'first Chinese tapestry' had been woven, was in economic difficulties; so Oudry, who had become director of the Manufacture Royale in 1734 (with Nicolas Besnier), was co-opted. Beauvais became, as Voltaire said, 'le royaume d'Oudry' who designed many cartoons for it: the *Molière Comedies,* the *Country Amusements* and the *Verdures Fines.* These last, which are fine examples of the artificial Baroque style, had an immense success, equalled only by that of Boucher's Beauvais series. The 'second Chinese tapestry' is notable for the brilliant decoration of the weave. After the deaths of Besnier and Oudry, Beauvais produced the *Russian Games* by Le Prince, *Country Amusements* by Casanova (1772) and the airy *Pastorals* of Huet. Tapestries from the Beauvais workshops bear the trademark 'B' and the fleur-de-lys of France.

Many of the series from Beauvais were repeated also at Aubusson (trademarks: M.R.D., M.R.D.A. or M.R.D.B.) with a more simplified technique, though still suitable for the Arcadian or pastoral themes. At the Gobelins works, but chiefly at Beauvais and Aubusson, tapestry covers for furniture were also woven in which fantasy and skill were well combined.

THE DECLINE OF FLEMISH SUPREMACY

In countries other than France the pictorial element had triumphed—and this was not simply in imitation of French taste. The 'Tenières' were in great demand in Brussels, although allegorical series (the *Seasons*, the *Months*, the *Four Continents*, from designs by L. van Schoor) as well as mythological and biblical scenes (the *History of Telemachus*, the *History of Moses*, from designs by Jan van Orley) were still being woven. The technical quality was still good, but production ran into increasing difficulties. 'Tenières' were being woven in other cities such as Lille, but there were plenty of rival subjects. The old workshops closed one after the other, and in the last quarter of the century only van der Borcht's remained. When Jacques van der Borcht died in 1794, even this was closed so that for the first time in nearly five hundred years, the sound of looms at work was no longer heard in Brussels.

Flanders had lost its supremacy in the craft of weaving—partly as a result of French competition, and partly because in the 18th century there was scarcely a country in Europe which did not boast at least one tapestry works.

In England until 1727 John Vanderbank of Soho was weaving *chinoiserie* tapestries with dark backgrounds, imitating lacquer—works of great elegance.

A whole colony of French weavers flourished in Germany—at Munich, and in Berlin where in 1699 Jean Barraban I and his brother-in-law Pierre

Mercier (who had earlier been in Berne) were at work. Starting with the *History of the Great Elector* (Schlossmuseum, Berlin), work was continued under Jean Barraban II and his colleague, Charles Vigne, with *Grotesque Inventions.* The elegant *Commedia dell'Arte* series (*c.* 1740–1745; Charlottenburg, Berlin) is attributed to Vigne alone.

French weavers also set up looms in Dresden, Schwabach, Erlangen and Würzburg. It is not surprising that the *Burlesques* woven at Würzburg by Pirot (*c.* 1740–1745; Residenz, Würzburg) were inspired by Tiepolo; they have something of his personal quality, although distorted by a certain mannerism and a striving for the picturesque.

18th-CENTURY ITALIAN TAPESTRIES

The Closing of the Medician Tapestry Workshops

Italy had long possessed her own tapestry traditions, enriched in the 18th century by the return, in 1703, of Termini. On arrival in Florence, he at once asked a clearly Rococo painter, Sagrestani, for cartoons. In the *Four Quarters of the Globe* his designs were well interpreted by the weavers, Leonardo Bernini and Vittorio Demignot. An exquisite range of soft and mellow tints creates the luminous effect of mother-of-pearl and gives them an unusual richness. After these came the *Elements,* begun with the four *portières,* from cartoons mostly by Sagrestani; they were to form a series of great tapestries with allusive mythological subjects, a style which still endured in Florence! Only two were woven—the *Rape of Proserpine* (designed by Grisoni) and the *Fall of Phaeton* (designed by Vincenzo Meucci). They are penetrated with a curious undulating light which seems to shroud the protagonists. The *Fall of Phaeton* was completed in 1737, the year in which, on the death of Gian Gastone, the Medici dynasty ended. The tapestry works did not survive him.

Papal Tapestry Workshops

There were still other workshops in Italy—the Ospizio di S. Michele a Ripa in Rome, for example, founded in 1710 by Pope Clement XI Albani, who appointed the French weaver, Signoret, as director, and the painter, Andrea Procaccini, as chief designer. In 1717 Pietro Ferloni became director and held the post until 1770. The production was very varied—sacred themes treated in cycles (and often inspired by paintings), portraits, holy pictures, minor decorative themes, copies of ancient tapestries, and wooded landscapes with figures. The workshop of S. Michele a Ripa was closed in 1798.

Turin

The restoration of the Turin royal palace in 1730 by Filippo Juvara undoubtedly contributed to the establishment of a tapestry workshop at the court of Savoy. Tapestries were needed to complete the decoration of the new apartments in keeping with their style and taste. It was clear therefore that Claudio Beaumont, who had decorated some of the rooms with frescoes should be asked to submit designs. Recalled from Florence in 1731, Demignot immediately opened a low-warp workshop. Its official inauguration did not take place until 1737, when a high-warp workshop was added; this was directed by Antonio Dini. Claudio Beaumont designed the *History of Alexander,* the *History of Caesar,* the *History of Hannibal* and the *History of Cyrus* (Palazzo Reale, Turin, and Quirinale, Rome) with heroic themes, which were most unusual in 18th-century tapestries. Unusual too was the form in which they were represented, adhering to the principle that a series of tapestries should be monumental, covering a whole wall, adapted organically to the architecture. The result was a compromise between ancient and modern. The large tapestries, of elaborate and stiff design, revealed mostly the influence of the traditional cartoons (above all, the various series of Le Brun), while the smaller panels, later episodes in a more liberal composition, are much richer in detail and more modern in style.

The *History of Cyrus* (*c.* 1750–1756) is hinted at rather than narrated, and deals only with the high points of the story; it is one of Beaumont's most felicitous works.

More suitable than the 'heroic' series in the taste of the period are the 'lesser' series at Turin, the marine and the architectural subjects, from designs by Francesco Antoniani. In the architecture series the notion of the 'woven wall' reaches its apogee of absurdity in a fanciful vision of ruins. Antoniani was responsible also for the designs for wooded landscapes with figures. Other designers were Angela Palanca and Vittorio Amedeo Cignaroli (after 1755), who, while still maintaining the conventions of the Arcadian idyll, introduced mellow rustic effects. The disturbing events at the end of the century caused the closing of the workshops. Between 1823, when they reopened, and 1832 they had little success.

French Influence in Naples

A workshop was opened at Naples in 1737 by Charles III; it gave work to the weavers who had lost their jobs with the closing of the Medici tapestry works. Their first series were the *Elements* for the royal palace at Caserta (1746) and other works imitating painting. In 1757 Pietro Duranti became director, and in the following year the vast *Don Quixote* series was begun; it was copied exactly from the series of the same name woven at the Gobelins, with only slight variations in the central subjects (some designed by Bonito).

That the dominant influence at Naples was French is confirmed in the *History of Henry IV*. Although the choice of the episodes is different, it is very similar to the series on the same subject woven at the Gobelins (1785–1786). The series marks the decline of the ornate Rococo style and the birth of a new historical and didactic manner. Its aesthetic content was

47. *The History of Psyche. The Banquet of Psyche* (detail).
Paris. First quarter of the 17th century. Bargello, Florence.

48. *Children Gardening. Winter.* Gobelins. Late 17th century, Mobilier National, Paris.

49. *The History of Alexander. Alexander in Darius's Tent.*
Gobelins. Late 17th century. Mobilier National, Paris.

50. *Royal Palaces. Vincennes*. Gobelins. Late 17th century.
Mobilier National, Paris.

51. *The History of Constantine. Victory engraving the Name of Constantine on the Shield.* Rome. 1639-1641. Private Collection, Milan.

52. *Putti at Play. The Game of Bowls.* Rome. 1633-1642.
Palazzo Venezia, Rome.

53. *Grotesques* (detail). Beauvais. Late 17th centur
Louvre, Par

54. *The Turkish Embassy. Leaving the Tuileries Gardens.*
Gobelins. 1734-1737. Mobilier National, Paris.

55. *The New Indies. The King carried in his Hammock.*
Gobelins. Mid 18th century. Mobilier National, Paris.

56. Second 'Chinese' tapestry. *The Flower Market*. Beauvais. 1743-1753. Palazzo Reale, Turin.

57. *Country Amusements. The Drinking Pool.* Beauvais.
1773-1779. Mobilier National, Paris.

58. *Rest during a Shoot* (detail). Second half 18th century.
Petit Palais, Paris.

59. *Landscape with Fox*. Oudenaarde. 18th century. Musées Royaux d'Art et d'Histoire, Brussels.

60. *The Flight into Egypt.* Rome. *c.* 1725. Vatican Museum, Rome.

61. Series of furniture coverings. Beauvais. 1815-1830.
Mobilier National, Paris.

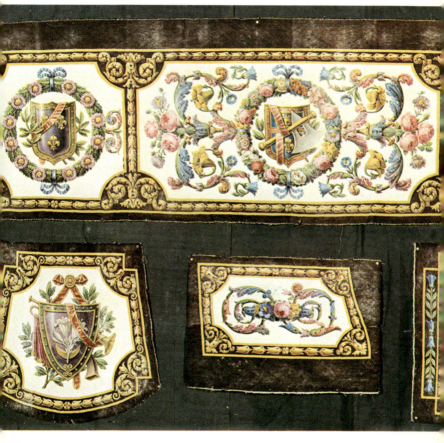

62. Design by Jean Lurçat. Aubusson, Paris. Musée d'Art Moderne, Paris.

meagre in both Paris and Naples (where work ceased in 1798).

THE DECLINE OF 18TH-CENTURY TAPESTRY

Towards the end of the century all the tapestry workshops found themselves in difficulties. The 1760s had marked new trends in culture and decoration; now the frivolous disenchanted century suddenly became serious, and caprice was replaced by reason. Modern culture was replaced by the classical world, not in the old tradition of the Renaissance or the Baroque, but as revealed by newly discovered originals.

Still influenced by designs which were now out of date, the art of tapestry could not adapt itself to the changes (it was not enough to abandon, as in the Gobelins, the elaborate cartoons of the surrounds). When the attempt was made, it produced works of poor quality, such as the *History of Henry IV*, although it occasionally achieved something thanks to the genius of an individual artist. Spanish tapestry was an example. The Real Fábrica de Tapices y Alfombras was established in Madrid by Philip IV in 1720, who summoned master weavers from Antwerp, headed by Jacob van der Goten. The first tapestries were 'Tenières' and hunting scenes (1723–1724), which were followed by the spirited *Don Quixote* series, designed by Andrea Procaccini. Other series were inspired by paintings—those of Amigoni (the *Four Seasons*), and of Giaquinto and Luca Giordano (the

Story of Joseph, the *Story of Solomon* and the *Story of David*). In 1762 Mengs was appointed director, and he commissioned cartoons from various artists. Among these was Bayeu who in 1776 gave Goya his first commission for tapestry designs. From 1777 to 1790 Goya designed no less than forty-three cartoons of contemporary village and country life. These form a large proportion of *Los Tapices* (Madrid).

This was a breath of fresh air; but no more than that for, except for the rare influence of one or two highly talented individual artists, it failed to liberate the art of tapestry from the dead hand of the 'picturesque'. In any case, times had changed too much for even a Goya to have the influence of a Raphael or a Rubens. The art of tapestry suffered from the revolutions and the wars, and was involved like everything else in the general European holocaust. Later, still bound by its outworn traditions, it could absorb nothing from the new ideas and emotions of its contemporaries.

During the French Revolution some of the most beautiful royal tapestries were burnt in order to yield their meagre gold content. This deplorable action had a symbolic value. It meant the end of a certain way of life, the collapse of a society which had attributed a mystical and evocative, as well as an artistic, value to the art of tapestry. It had become identified with the decorative luxury, power and dignity of the Sovereign and the aristocracy. When the *History of Scipio* by Giulio Romano and the *Seasons* by Charles Le Brun were burnt, the world they represented was destroyed with them.

TAPESTRY TODAY

It was stated at the outset that tapestry is now a contemporary art; this renaissance is an accomplished fact, visible in contemporary society. But is it truly a phoenix, arisen from its old ashes? It has arisen, but in a totally different form. The public today wants something different. Its artists are quite different from those of the past—a salutary factor, for it would otherwise be no more than a sterile resuscitation of something long dead. William Morris's attempt at the end of the 19th century to revive the art as it was in its medieval heyday was admirable, less for his return to that period than because he became insensibly associated with the 'modern style' of woven panels. In our own century the work of Lurçat, the great exponent of the tapestry renaissance in France, is known more for his decorative effects, obtained by a cubistic treatment of space, than for any attempts at returning to the technicalities of the medieval manner. His influence has affected contemporary artists as well as the public, and he has shown that an ancient art can still be interpreted in the modern spirit. An examination of the catalogues of the two tapestry exhibitions in Lausanne (1964, 1966) shows that his influence is not confined to France alone, and that tapestries of great variety and expression are being woven all over the world.

To sum up, the art of tapestry is still alive in a new renaissance, inheriting the traditions of the past and looking confidently to the future.

LIST OF ILLUSTRATIONS

1.   Cloth of St Gereon (fragment). Cologne. 11th century. Musée des Tissus, Lyon. The cloth of St Gereon has typical design motifs. The inclusion of ornamental motifs in the comprehensive framing reveals a first, if tentative, attempt at variety.

2.   *Apocalypse of St John. The Fifth Angel.* Designer, Hennequin de Bruges; weaver, Nicolas Bataille. Paris. Last quarter of the 14th century. Musée des Tapisseries, Angers. The scenes are set in squares, on two levels. A remarkable knowledge of decoration is united to absolute simplicity and a sense of expression, creating a perfectly coherent style.

3.   *Apocalypse of St John. St Michael and the Devil.* Designer, Hennequin de Bruges; weaver, Nicolas Bataille. Paris. Last quarter of the 14th century. Musée des Tapisseries, Angers. The *Apocalypse*, which was known as the *'beau tapis'* of Louis of Anjou, presented considerable difficulties never before confronted by the designer and the weavers, not the least difficulty being its correlation with contemporary painting.

4.   *The Presentation in the Temple* (detail). Paris. Third quarter of the 14th century. Musées Royaux d'Art et d'Histoire, Brussels. This fragment, at one time part of a much larger tapestry, is on account of the strong similarities in the weaving of the *Apocalypse* attributed to the studio of Nicolas Bataille.

5.   *History of St Piat and St Eleuthère. St Eleuthère raising the Tribune's Daughter from the Dead.* Weaver, Pierrot Féré. Arras. 1402. Tournai cathedral. The only documented tapestry at Arras, a precedent for the attribution of contemporary work. Notable for its realism and humanity, rather than for any courtly or chivalrous element.

6.   *The Offering of the Heart.* Arras. Beginning of the 15th century. Musée des Arts Décoratifs, Paris. The fragment, probably illustrating some chivalric romance is attributed with good reason to the school of Arras. The design is elegant, and the weave is similar technically to that of the *History of St Piat and St Eleuthère*.

7.   *Story of Alexander the Great*. Episode in a battle (detail). Weaver, Pasquier Grenier. Tournai. 1459. Doria Pamphili Collection, Rome. This panel is believed to have formed part of the *'chambre'* acquired by Philip the Good from Grenier in 1459. The episodes with their densely crowded figures, were taken from the *Livre des Conquestes et faicts d'Alexandre le Grand* by J. Wauquelin

8.   *The Legend of Herkenbald* (detail). *Trajan's Justice*. Tournai. Before 1461. Historisches Museum, Berne. This tapestry, with the arms of Bishop Giorgio di Saluzzo (d. 1461) was inspired by the paintings of van der Weyden and interpreted in a highly stylised manner. The play of light is ingeniously varied, now subdued, now vibrating.

9.   *The Ball of the Savages* (detail). Tournai? *c.* mid 15th century. Musée des Arts Décoratifs, Saumur. At Tournai we find the same sustained and insistent rhythm of the composite weft, the same cohesive stylisation of figures, the same decoration, all combining to form a monumental 'mural' compactness.

10.   Floral Tapestry with the arms of Philip the Good. Brussels. 1466. Weaver, Jean de Haze. Historisches Museum, Berne. The 'thousand flowers' are skilfully drawn on the background, with great attention to nature. This panel has recently been attributed to Brussels.

11.   *Wild Man with the Unicorn*. The upper Rhine. First quarter of the 15th century. Museum of Fine Arts, Boston. This tapestry is dominated by an ornamental extravagance with no regard for nature. The popular legend here becomes simply a pretext for decoration.

12.   *Wild Woman with the Unicorn*. The upper Rhine. Last quarter of the 15th century. Historisches Museum, Basle. The stylisation of Swiss tapestries is here redeemed by a sense of fantasy and good taste.

13. *The Virgin in Glory*. Brussels. 1489. Louvre, Paris. This tapestry, one of the first which can be reasonably attributed to the Brussels studio, is believed to have been designed by the Maître des Feuillages en Broderie. This inspiration is confirmed by comparison with the general composition of a small altar-piece by this same master. The delicate execution marks it as intended to be a 'painting in a tapestry'.

14. *The Communion of Herkenbald*. Designer, Jan van Roome; weaver, Maître Lyon (Léon de Smet?). Brussels. 1513. Musées Royaux d'Art et d'Histoire, Brussels. This tapestry was commissioned by the Confraternity of the Holy Sacraments of Louvain. It was completed in 1513 by a certain Maître Lyon, who wove it from a design by Jan van Roome, enlarged into a cartoon by Maitre Philippe. It is a typical example of the Brussels style.

15. *The Last Supper* (detail). Brussels. 1516. Museo d'Arte Sacra, Camaiore. This tapestry is among the few from the first quarter of the 16th century. It has been attributed to the studio of Pieter Pannemaker (after comparison with the *History of David* in the Musée de Cluny). We know from a letter of Maximilian of Austria that Pannemaker was already at work in 1517. The theme of *The Last Supper* was certainly used by him later (1531) in a tapestry for the Emperor Charles V.

16.   *Descent from the Cross*. Brussels. First quarter of the 16th century. Milan cathedral. This is related to a whole group of Brussels tapestries, without being exactly in the style of van Roome. It differs from his work as being both more sentimental and deeper in feeling.

17.   *Descent from the Cross* (detail). Brussels. First quarter of the 16th century. Milan cathedral. The exaggerated sentimentality of the subject, which is pathetic rather than dramatic, does not affect the spectacular richness of the weaving. Gold is employed for the superimposed embroidery.

18.   *Esther and Ahasuerus*. Brussels. First quarter of the 16th century. Poldi Pezzoli Museum, Milan. The subtlety of the weaving is here ingeniously adapted to the requirements of the drapery. The importance lies not in the conventionally graceful figures, but in the magnificent brocades of the woven garments, which are highly decorated.

19. *La Dame à la Licorne. The Unicorn and the Mirror.* Brussels. *c.* 1480–1490. Musée de Cluny, Paris. The origin of this famous series was for long uncertain. If the new attribution to Brussels is, as it seems, correct, its style is connected with the aristocratic type of tapestry with millefleurs background.

20. *Feudal Life. The Bath.* French tapestry (?) of the end of the 15th century, Musée de Cluny, Paris. Tapestry of uncertain origin. The feudal spirit it reflects appears to be the result of a deliberate fidelity to an ideal felt genuinely as a valid creative inspiration.

21. *The Triumphs of Petrarch. The Triumph of Time over Fame* (detail). Flemish. End of the 15th century. Kunsthistorisches Museum, Vienna. The origin of this series is uncertain, appearing to be either from Tournai or from some other Flemish centre. The cultured emblematic and literary subject, with its sometimes abstruse symbolism, is woven into the tapestry with clear and decorative effect.

22.   *The Triumphs of Petrarch. The Triumph of Death over Chastity* (detail showing Pandora). Flemish. End of 15th century. Kunsthistorisches Museum, Vienna. The *Triumphs* reveal wide and varied culture both in their exquisite details and the composition as a whole. Light and flowing, it seems to have been designed to illustrate the poetry of Petrarch.

23.   *Christ's Passion. The Last Supper.* Venice. *c.* 1420–1430. S. Marco, Venice. This series was probably woven in Venice by weavers from the north, who—and this is documented—worked there at the time. This explains the mixture, in the panels, of northern and Lombard methods.

24.   *Christ's Passion. Christ before Pilate.* Venice. *c.* 1420–1430. S. Marco, Venice. In the *Passion*, the limitations of the scenes and the alternating colours of the backgrounds recall illustrated manuscripts. This would account for the mirror inversion of the scenes owing to the weave (high warp) in which the weaver stands behind the tapestry and must view his work in a looking-glass.

25. *The Months. December.* Cartoon by Bramantino; weaver, Benedetto da Milano. Vigevano. *c.* 1503. Castello Sforzesco, Milan. The attribution to Bramantino is contested; but only an artist of great quality could have produced such a combination of noble figures to match the aesthetic values of the Renaissance composition.

26. *The Acts of the Apostles. The Miraculous Draught of Fishes.* Cartoon by Raphael; weavers, J. van Tiegen and J. van Herselle. Brussels. *c.* 1540. Palazzo Ducale, Mantua. These cartoons caused great excitement in the studios of Brussels. Raphael has combined inimitably both pure decoration and monumental grandeur.

27. *The Acts of the Apostles. St Peter healing the Cripple.* Cartoon by Raphael; weavers, J. van Tiegen and J. van Herselle. Brussels. *c.* 1540. Palazzo Ducale, Mantua. These cartoons are not all by Raphael. Giulio Romano, Penni, and G. da Udine had a part in the design. But they reflect the classical ideal of Raphael.

28. *Story of Genesis. The Expulsion of Adam and Eve from the Garden of Eden.* Designer, Michiel Coxcie. Brussels. Mid 16th century. Accademia, Florence. Coxcia, although inspired by formal Italian traditions, still retained a basic Flemish tone which is particularly noticeable in his attention to natural details.

29. *The Battle of Pavia. The Cavalry Charge.* Designer, B. van Orley; weaver, J. Gheetels. Brussels. *c.* 1530. Museo di Capodimonte, Naples. The designer reveals exceptional ability in his portrayal of contemporary decoration and the solemnity fitting the occasion.

30. *The History of St George and St Maurelius. St George Slays the Dragon.* Designers, B. Tisi, C. Filippo, L. d'Olanda; weaver, J. Carcher. Ferrara. 1552–1553. Ferrara cathedral. The seven tapestries commissioned by the cathedral are dated and signed 'G. Carcher'.

31. *Putti at Play*. *The Arbour*. Designer Giulio Romano; weaver, Jan Carcher? Ferrara? *c*. 1540–1545. Museo Poldi Pezzoli, Milan. This series is attributed, probably correctly, to Giulio Romano, whose cartoons and preparatory drawings are known.

32. *The History of Moses*. *The Brazen Serpent*. Weaver, Jan or Nicolaus Carcher. Ferrara or Mantua. After 1550? Milan cathedral. This series (at one time six tapestries of which now only three survive) originally formed part of the 'eight pieces of silk and gold thread given by the Duke of Mantua' to St Charles Borromeo before 1566. The arms of Guglielmo Gonzaga also appear.

33. *The History of Joseph*. *Joseph repulsing Potiphar's Wife*. Designer, A. Bronzino; weaver, N. Carcher. Florence. 1549. Palazzo Vecchio, Florence. According to Vasari, 'the flight of Joseph leaving his shirt in the hands of Potiphar's wife' was designed by Pontormo. Nevertheless, the style of Bronzino, who sought a compromise between 'relief' and 'capricious inventions', is reflected in this tapestry.

34.   *Ecce Homo*. Designer, F. Salviati; weaver, N. Carcher. Florence. 1549. Uffizi Gallery, Florence. In this and other small tapestries, Salviati reveals great stylistic virtuosity. The same may be said for his larger works.

35.   *The Months. June and July* (detail of the *June* Harvest). Designer, F. Ubertini, called il Bachiacca; weaver, G. Rost. Florence, 1553. Uffizi Gallery, Florence. The elegant series is woven from precious materials. Taking into account the dimensions and the extremely detailed technique, it is probable that the *Months* were destined for a room in the grand-ducal apartments.

36.   *The Hunts. Hunting the Wild Cat*. Designer, G. Stradanus; weaver, B. Squilli. Florence. 1577. Palazzo Vecchio, Florence. In these *Hunts*, ordered for the Medici villa of Poggio a Cajano, Stradanus combines great narrative ability with a feeling for rural life. Although the northern tradition is apparent here, southern tradition had at another period an influence on Flanders.

37. *Landscape with a Hunt*. Weaver, F. Guebels and an unidentified colleague. Brussels. Last quarter of the 16th century. Museo Civico, Turin. This tapestry, bearing the arms of Ferrero Fieschi di Masserano, is a typical example of the taste of the Brussels weavers towards the end of the 16th century. The background is covered by massed foliage, while the figures are of secondary importance.

38. *The History of Orlando Furioso* (detail). Weaver, F. Spierinck. Delft. Early 17th century. Museo Poldi Pezzoli, Milan. Although related to the contemporary taste for hunting scenes and wooded landscapes, this tapestry is notable for its mannered elegance, fine weaving and unusual subject.

39. *The History of Troy. Duel between two Warriors*. Oudenaarde. Late 16th century. Private Collection, Venice. This tapestry is part of a series which used to hang in the castle of Verzuolo, near Saluzzo. The treatment, summary and simplified, is a mixture of hunting scenes and wooded landscapes. It expresses in archaic style both legend and the age of chivalry.

40. *Altarpiece of the Doge Marino Grimani*. Designer A. Allori. Florence. 1595. S. Marco, Venice. This altarpiece is based on an older one (1571) of the Doge Mocenigo. The extreme richness of the materials in the weave, which in other cases might detract from the stiffness of the style, here serves to enhance the obsession for panels.

41. *The Triumph of the Eucharist. The Miraculous Fall of Manna* (detail). Designer P. P. Rubens. Brussels. Mid 17th century. Palazzo Reale, Turin. A typical composition of Rubens, where even the 'minor' figures play their part. The movement and gestures of the Hebrews collecting the manna combine something both of the biblical patriarch and the heroes of mythology.

42. *The History of Achilles. Achilles and the Centaur Chiron*. Designer J. Jordaens; weaver, J. F. van der Hecke. Brussels. Mid 17th century. Palazzo Reale, Turin. The series is from designs by Rubens and Jordaens. In the tapestry here reproduced there is a clear relaxation of the dramatic tension of Rubens' exalted style, to the advantage of the delightful narrative sense.

43. *The History of Aurelian and Zenobia. Zenobia as a Prisoner.* Designer, J. van Egmont; weaver, G. Peemans. Brussels. End of the 17th century. Musées Royaux d'Art et d'Histoire, Brussels. The story of the love of Aurelian and Zenobia is related in a theatrical series which is both decorative and full of interesting detail. A pictorial 'curiosity'.

44. *The Liberal Arts. The Grammar Lesson.* Bruges. *c.* 1665. Castello Sforzesco, Milan. In the 17th century Bruges produced a number of tapestries, in which the liberal arts were freely interpreted from a series of engravings by Cornelius Schut.

45. *The History of Artemisia. Mounted Heralds.* Studio of de La Planche and Comans. Paris. *c.* 1625. Mobilier National, Paris. This vast series contains subjects such as the *Mounted Heralds* which have little to do with the story; they are descriptive interludes.

46. *The History of Diana. Diana refusing to marry Otus.* Designer, T. Dubreuil. Studio of de La Planche and Comans. Paris. *c.* 1625. Palazzo Reale, Turin. Expressed in a somewhat archaic style, the free narrative manner lends charm to the picture.

47. *The History of Psyche. The Banquet of Psyche* (detail). Weavers, M. Dubourg, G. Laurent. Louvre, Paris. First quarter of the 17th century. Bargello, Florence. In 1551 Henry II of France founded an institution at the Trinité where orphans were taught to weave tapestries. In 1608 Maurice Dubourg, trained at the Trinité, moved with his associate, Laurent, into a studio in the Louvre. *The History of Psyche*, woven there, was an adaptation to tapestry of decorative pictures by Coxcie.

48. *Children Gardening. Winter.* Designer, C. Le Brun. Gobelins. Late 17th century. Mobilier National, Paris. The series of *Children Gardening,* of which the first was woven in 1685 (but designed much earlier), is characteristic of the designer Le Brun's considered and reflective style. It was based on a 16th-century theme, of *Putti at Play*, which had been used in Italy so successfully for tapestry by Giovanni da Udine and Giulio Romano.

49. *The History of Alexander. Alexander in Darius's Tent.* Designer, C. Le Brun. Gobelins. Late 17th century. Mobilier National, Paris. Recourse to an illusive depth, more suggestive than realistic in the spectacular design of the tent, is typical of Le Brun's composition, then almost an innovation. The parallel between Alexander and Louis XIV is so subtly suggested as to recall the transposition of subjects and figures in the contemporary 'ballets de cour'.

50. *Royal Palaces. Vincennes.* Designers, C. Le Brun and A. Genoels. Gobelins. Late 17th century. Mobilier National, Paris. The principal subject, the gloomy castle of Vincennes, appears in the background, surrounded by an architectural framework of cornices; on one side they enhance the royal dignity, while on the other they produce the sense of a 'picture' with its panoramic vista.

51. *The History of Constantine. Victory engraving the Name of Constantine on the Shield.* Designer, Pietro da Cortona; weaver, G. Rocci. Barberini studio, Rome. 1639–1641. Private collection, Milan. The classical inspiration of this series by Pietro da Cortona, continuing Rubens's *History of Constantine,* is evident. This decoration round the doorway seems inspired by medallions, an impression confirmed by the use of grisaille.

52. *Putti at Play*. *The Game of Bowls*. Designer, G. F. Romanelli; weaver, G. della Riviera. Barberini studio, Rome. 1633–1642. Palazzo Venezia, Rome. The lost series of *Putti at Play* by Giovanni da Udine inspired Romanelli. But it was no more than inspiration, for here he seems determined above all to introduce a light Baroque atmosphere of airy illusion and a feeling of space.

53. *Grotesques* (detail). Designer, J. B. Monnoyer. Beauvais. Late 17th century. Louvre, Paris. Designed by Bérain before 1689 and made into cartoons by Monnoyer, this bizarre series announces the new era of 18th-century taste.

54. *The Turkish Embassy*. *Leaving the Tuileries Gardens*. Designer, C. Parrocel. Gobelins. 1734–1737. Mobilier National, Paris. The series was woven to commemorate the entry of the Turkish ambassador, Mehmet Effendi, into Paris in 1721. The event was doubly interesting for the French, as the taste for the exotic was becoming fashionable at this time.

55. *The New Indies. The King carried in his Hammock.* Cartoon, F. Desportes. Gobelins. Mid 18th century. Mobilier National, Paris. The first series of the *Indies* was set up on the Gobelins looms in 1687, taken from paintings by the Dutch artist Albert Eckhout. In 1737 Desportes invested the exotic illustrations with subtle overtones.

56. Second 'Chinese' tapestry. *The Flower Market.* Cartoon, F. Boucher; weaver, N. Besniers. Beauvais. 1743–1753. Palazzo Reale, Turin. That a taste for *chinoiserie* influenced 17th- and 18th-century tapestry weaving is proved by the first 'Chinese' tapestry, woven at Beauvais. Boucher took up the subject and added the grace and sensuality of his own style.

57. *Country Amusements. The Drinking Pool.* Designer, F. Casanova. Beauvais. 1773–1779. Mobilier National, Paris. In this series of Arcadian pastoral idylls Rococo taste is still very evident, although at this time throughout Europe a very different style of art was emerging, classical or at least inclined towards the antique, a tendency which the workshops were late in recognising.

58. *Rest during a Shoot* (detail). Aubusson. Second half 18th century. Petit Palais, Paris. The 18th-century Aubusson tapestries obtained pleasing effects, especially with country scenes set in artificial landscapes.

59. *Landscape with Fox*. Oudenaarde. 18th century. Musées Royaux d'Art et d'Histoire, Brussels. Tapestries from Oudenaarde had some success in the 18th century, in particular their fine landscapes packed with foliage and animals, woven in dull greens occasionally relieved by a vivid touch of colour. This is part of a series for a private house in Brussels.

60. *The Flight into Egypt*. Ospizio di S. Michele a Ripa, Rome. *c.* 1725. Vatican Museum, Rome. This form of pictorial tapestry is similar to that of the 18th-century wooded landscape, then much in fashion. It is in a strange technique with its trite combinations of colours, giving the appearance of an embroidery.

61. Series of furniture coverings. Designer, Saint-Ange. Beauvais. 1815–1830. Mobilier National, Paris. The production of tapestries to cover furniture flourished during the 18th century, particularly at Beauvais. The 19th-century examples by Saint-Ange reveal the continuing excellence of the craftsmen and their ability to adapt themselves.

62. Design by Jean Lurçat. Aubusson, Paris. Musée d'Art Moderne, Paris. The aesthetic ideas of Lurçat are woven on to canvas by a method of his own. The use of gros point is reintroduced for contrasted decorative effects. Nature is lyrically treated.